WHO WAS...?

Queen Victoria

Dereen Taylor

First published in 2007 by Wayland

This paperback edition published in 2009 by Wayland

Copyright © Wayland 2007

Wayland
338 Euston Road
London NW1 3BH

Wayland Australia
Level 17/207 Kent Street
Sydney, NSW 2000

Editor: Victoria Brooker
Designer: Jane Stanley

Taylor, Dereen
   Who was Queen Victoria?
   1. Victoria, Queen of Great Britain, 1819-1901 - Juvenile
literature 2. Great Britain - Kings and rulers - Biography
- Juvenile literature 3. Great Britain - History -
Victoria, 1837-1901 - Juvenile literature
   I. Title
   941'.081'092

ISBN 978 0 7502 5984 2

Printed in China

Wayland is a division of Hachette Children's Books, an Hachette UK Company.
www.hachette.co.uk

For permission to reproduce the following pictures, the author and publisher would like
to thank: Bettmann/Corbis: 18; Stefan Bianchetti/Corbis: 19; City Museums & Art
Gallery, Plymouth, Devon, UK/Bridgeman Art Library, London: 20; Mary Evans Picture
Library: 7, 12, 21; Getty Images (Hulton Archive): 6, 13, 16, 17; Private Collection/
Bridgeman Art Library, London: 11 Private Collection/©Archives Charmet/Bridgeman
Art Library: 4, Cover; Private Collection/Photo©Christie's Images/Bridgeman Art
Library, London: 8; Private Collection/©Dreweatt Neate Fine Art Auctioneers, Newbury,
Berks, UK/Bridgeman Art Library, London: 9; Private Collection/©Look and Learn/
Bridgeman Art Library, London: 14; Topham Picturepoint/TopFoto: 5; Victoria & Albert
Museum, London/Sally Chappell/The Art Archive: 10; Laurie Platt Winfrey/The Art
Archive: 15

Contents

Words in **bold** can be found in the glossary.

Who was Queen Victoria?

Queen Victoria ruled over Britain and the **British Empire** from 1837 to 1901. She was Queen for 64 years. This was the longest **reign** of any British king or queen.

This portrait of Queen Victoria was painted in 1887.

This photograph is of a middle-class Victorian family at home. It was taken towards the end of Victoria's reign in 1889.

Places to Visit

Buckingham Palace. Queen Victoria was the first British **monarch** to live there. Today it is the London home of Queen Elizabeth II.

We call people who lived at that time Victorians. The Victorians liked the royal family and crowds came to see Queen Victoria wherever she went.

Victoria's childhood

Queen Victoria was born in 1819. She was the only child of Prince Edward and his German wife, Princess Victoria.

Victoria's mother called her daughter by a special name, 'Drina', when the two of them were together.

Victoria's father died when she was a baby. She grew up in Kensington Palace in London with her mother.

Victoria didn't go to school with other children. Instead, she was taught German, French, history and maths at home. The young Victoria enjoyed singing and painting.

As a girl Victoria had lessons on her own with her teacher.

Places to Visit

Kensington Palace, London. There is a large statue of Queen Victoria in front of the palace. It was sculpted by Victoria's daughter, Princess Louise, to celebrate Queen Victoria's Golden Jubilee in 1887.

Heir to the throne

Victoria's uncle, King William IV, had no children. This meant Victoria was **heir** to the British throne. When William IV died in 1837, Victoria became Queen of Great Britain and Ireland. She was just eighteen years old.

This portrait shows Queen Victoria in her **coronation** robes. She is about to wear the royal crown for the first time.

Her coronation was a year later at Westminster Abbey. Thousands of coronation souvenirs were sold to celebrate this important event.

VICTORIA REGINA.
Crowned 28th of June 1838.
Born 24th May 1819. Proclaimed 20th of June 1837.

The British people rushed out to buy coronation souvenirs. This was a way of showing their support for the young Queen.

Victoria and Albert

In 1840, when Victoria was 21, she married Prince Albert. He was her German cousin. Victoria listened to Albert's advice and he helped her do her job as Queen.

Victoria and Albert were very happily married and enjoyed spending time together.

In 1851 Prince Albert organised the Crystal Palace Exhibition. This was a huge fair that showed off the best **inventions** from around the world.

The Crystal Palace Exhibition in 1851 showed the world the achievements of the **British Empire**.

Sons and daughters

Queen Victoria and Prince Albert had a happy life together. They had nine children — four sons and five daughters. They were called Victoria, Albert Edward, Alice, Alfred, Helena, Louise, Arthur, Leopold and Beatrice.

This family photograph of Queen Victoria and Prince Albert with their children was taken in about 1860.

Through the marriages of her children and grandchildren, Queen Victoria was related to many royal families in Europe. She was sometimes known as 'The Grandmother of Europe'.

Victoria and Albert made the German custom of Christmas trees popular in Britain.

Victorian inventions

Queen Victoria's **reign** also saw the arrival of many important **inventions**. The **engineer** Isambard Kingdom Brunel built railway bridges and tunnels, which are still used today. The first car powered by petrol instead of steam went on sale to the public in 1884.

Places to Visit

You can see many Victorian inventions at the Science Museum in London.

Queen Victoria made her first train journey on a steam train like this.

In 1876, the Scottish inventor Alexander Graham Bell invented the first telephone. In 1878, Queen Victoria used a telephone for the first time at Osborne House.

This photograph of Alexander Graham Bell shows him using his 'electrical speech machine'. We now call this invention the telephone.

Victoria in mourning

Queen Victoria's much loved husband Albert died from **typhoid** in 1861. Victoria was heartbroken and was not seen in public for over ten years.

After Albert's death, Queen Victoria always wore black to show how much she missed her husband.

She spent most of her time at Balmoral Castle in Scotland. This made Victoria unpopular with the Victorians. They wanted her to act like their Queen again.

IT'S TRUE!

After Albert's death, Victoria had a smaller crown made that sat on top of the veil she always wore.

Prince Albert had bought Balmoral Castle as a gift for the Queen in 1852.

The British Empire

During the **reign** of Queen Victoria, Britain ruled countries all over the world. These countries belonged to the **British Empire**.

This cartoon appeared in a newspaper in 1876. It shows the Prime Minister, Benjamin Disraeli, making Queen Victoria Empress of India.

Britain was becoming richer and more successful. The countries in the Empire provided Britain with food and **materials** such as cotton and rubber. British factories turned these materials into **goods** that were sold all over the world.

It was a long, hard day for these women working in a cotton factory in Derby.

Queen Victoria's death

Queen Victoria was seen again in public in 1887, for her Golden Jubilee. She had been Queen for 50 years.

This cup and saucer were made to celebrate the Queen's Golden Jubilee in 1887.

On 22 June 1897 it was the Queen's Diamond Jubilee. People marched through London to give thanks for Victoria's sixty years as Queen.

Queen Victoria died at Osborne House in 1901. For most people, Victoria had been a popular Queen and the only **monarch** they had ever known.

Places to Visit

St George's Chapel, Windsor Castle is where Queen Victoria's funeral was held in 1901. Queen Victoria and Prince Albert are both buried there.

This portrait shows the coffin of Queen Victoria being guarded by soldiers at Osborne House on the Isle of Wight.

Timeline

1819 Princess Alexandrina Victoria is born on 24 May

1837 Victoria becomes Queen on 20 June

1838 Queen Victoria's coronation at Westminster Abbey on 28 June

1840 Queen Victoria marries Prince Albert on 10 February

1851 Great Exhibition at Crystal Palace

1852 Prince Albert buys Balmoral Castle in Scotland for Queen Victoria

1861 Prince Albert dies on 14 December
      Queen Victoria goes into mourning

1876 Queen Victoria becomes Empress of India
      Scottish inventor Alexander Graham Bell invents the first telephone

1887 Queen Victoria's Golden Jubilee celebrating fifty years
      on the throne

1897 Queen Victoria's Diamond Jubilee celebrating sixty years
      on the throne

1901 Queen Victoria dies at Osborne House on 22 January
      Queen Victoria's eldest son becomes King Edward VII

Glossary

British Empire countries around the world under the rule of the British monarch

coronation the ceremony held when a new monarch is crowned king or queen

crowned to crown somebody is to give them the royal crown and make them king or queen of a country

engineer someone who makes machines, or plans the building of roads and bridges

goods things that can be bought and sold

heir someone who inherits a role or estate from another

invention a new object that has been created

materials anything solid that can be used to make something else. Cotton, rubber and wood are all materials

monarch another word for a king or queen

reign the period during which a king or queen rules

typhoid a serious infection that is caught from dirty food or water

Further information

Books

The Life and World of Queen Victoria by Brian Williams (Heinemann Library, 2002)

Famous People, Famous Lives: Queen Victoria by Harriet Castor (Franklin Watts, 2002)

Websites

http://www.bbc.co.uk/history/historic_figures/victoria_queen.shtml
A biography of Queen Victoria for use with teachers and parents.

http://www.bbc.co.uk/schools/victorians/
BBC schools website explores the life of children in Victorian times.

Index

Introduction

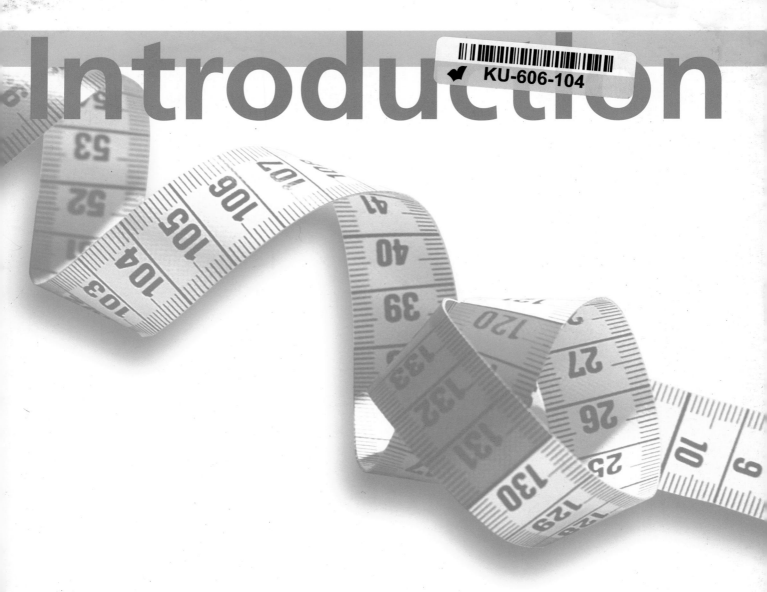

This workbook is designed to be used in conjunction with *The Essentials of AQA Maths – Linear Specification A (3301): Higher Tier*. It is matched page for page to this revision guide and consists of structured questions with spaces for answers, plus extension questions.

The contributors to this workbook are former or current GCSE examiners who have drawn on their experience to produce interesting and challenging exam-style questions. The worksheets are designed to reinforce understanding of the material in the revision guide, which is covered in the specification.

Details of our other AQA Maths Revision Guides and Workbooks can be found on the inside back cover.

Consultant Editor:
John Proctor B.Sc. (Hons), Cert. Ed.
Director of Specialist College,
St. Mary's Catholic High School,
Astley,
Manchester
(An 11-18 Specialist Mathematics and Computing College)

Editor:
Kay Chawner
Formerly a mathematics teacher at
The Ridgeway School, Swindon.

*Although this workbook is intended for candidates following the linear specification, it can also be used by candidates following the MODULAR B (3302) specification.

Contents

Place Value

1 Complete the following table. The first row has been done for you.

	Place Value of Digits					Number
	10 000 Ten Thousands	**1 000** Thousands	**100** Hundreds	**10** Tens	**1** Units	
			3	2	6	Three hundred and twenty six
a)		5	3	0	7	
b)	7	3	1	5	8	
c)						Five hundred and sixty
d)		1			7	, two hundred and forty
e)						Fourteen thousand and fifty two

2 Round 493 507 to the nearest...

a) 10 000 .... **b)** 1 000 .... **c)** 100 .... **d)** 10 ....

3 Round 109 109 to the nearest...

a) 10 000 .... **b)** 1 000 .... **c)** 100 .... **d)** 10 ....

4 If the attendance at a football match was 32 000 to the nearest thousand, what is the lowest possible number and the highest possible number of people that could have attended the match?

Lowest possible number: .... Highest possible number: ....

5 The number of boys who attended school on a particular day was 440 to the nearest ten. On the same day the number of girls who attended school was 460 to the nearest ten.

a) What is the lowest possible difference between the number of boys and the number of girls who attended school on that day? ....

....

b) What is the highest possible difference between the number of boys and the number of girls who attended? ....

....

6 Draw a table to show the place value of each digit in the following numbers:
a) one **b)** eighty seven **c)** four hundred and nine **d)** six thousand, two hundred and twenty three **e)** fifty thousand and five

7 Round 30 715 to the nearest...
a) thousand **b)** hundred **c)** ten

8 Write the equivalent value of 'a quarter of a million' in...
a) numbers **b)** words

4   NUMBER   Revision Guide Reference: Page 4   *Lonsdale* REVISION GUIDES

Rounding Numbers

1 Round ...

a) 7.321 to **i)** 1 decimal place .... **ii)** 2 decimal places ....

b) 16.781 to **i)** 1 decimal place .... **ii)** 2 decimal places ....

c) 0.01765 to **i)** 2 decimal places .... **ii)** 3 decimal places ....

d) 0.1053 to **i)** 1 decimal place .... **ii)** 3 decimal places ....

e) 7.0707 to **i)** 1 decimal place .... **ii)** 2 decimal places ....

2 Dave weighs 68.4kg to 1 decimal place. What is the lowest measurement and the highest measurement possible for his actual weight to 2 decimal places?

Lowest possible weight: .... Highest possible weight: ....

3 Helen's height is 1.65m to 2 decimal places. What is the lowest measurement and the highest measurement possible for her actual height to 3 decimal places?

Lowest possible height: .... Highest possible height: ....

4 Round...

a) 432 to **i)** 1 significant figure .... **ii)** 2 significant figures ....

b) 9 154 to **i)** 1 significant figure .... **ii)** 2 significant figures ....

c) 10 047 to **i)** 2 significant figures .... **ii)** 4 significant figures ....

d) 0.0238 to **i)** 1 significant figure .... **ii)** 2 significant figures ....

e) 0.0001736 to **i)** 2 significant figures .... **ii)** 3 significant figures ....

f) 0.010366 to **i)** 2 significant figures .... **ii)** 3 significant figures ....

5 The attendance at a pop concert was 5 700 to 2 significant figures. What is the difference between the lowest possible actual attendance and the highest possible actual attendance?

....

....

....

---

6 Round 135.6742 to ...
a) 1 decimal place **b)** 2 decimal places **c)** 1 significant figure **d)** 2 significant figures **e)** 3 significant figures

7 Round 0.06038 to ...
a) 1 decimal place **b)** 2 decimal places **c)** 3 decimal places **d)** 1 significant figure **e)** 2 significant figures **f)** 3 significant figures

8 Fran's weight to 1 decimal place is 47.6kg. What is the difference between her highest possible weight and her lowest possible weight to 2 decimal places?

9 **a)** Use your calculator to work out the value of $(1.46)^2 \times 6.71$. Write down all the digits on your display.
b) Round your answer to a suitable degree of accuracy.

Numbers 1 & 2

1 **Here are eight numbers:**

(3) (4) (6) (7) (11) (15) (20) (21)

a) Which three numbers are even numbers? ....

b) Which two numbers are factors of 40? ....

c) Which two numbers are factors of 45? ....

d) Which four numbers are factors of 42? ....

e) Which two numbers are multiples of 7? ....

f) Which three numbers are multiples of 2? ....

g) Which three numbers are prime numbers? ....

h) Which number has an odd number of factors? ....

2 **Here are ten numbers:**

(5) (8) (11) (19) (22) (24) (31) (36) (47) (81)

a) Which six numbers are odd numbers? ....

b) Which three numbers are factors of 72? ....

c) Which three numbers are factors of 110? ....

d) Which three numbers are multiples of 3? ....

e) Which three numbers are multiples of 4? ....

f) Which five numbers are prime numbers? ....

g) Which two numbers have an odd number of factors? ....

3 **What is the reciprocal of...**

a) 8? .... **b)** 25? .... **c)** 0.5? .... **d)** $\frac{3}{4}$? ....

4 **The reciprocal of a number is 0.1. What is the number?** ....

5 **Express the following numbers in prime factor form:**

a) 36 .... **b)** 64 .... **c)** 930 ....

6 **p and q are prime numbers: $p^2 q^3 = 72$**

Find the values of...   p ....   q ....

7 **a)** What is the highest common factor of 20 and 36?

....

....

....

....

b) What is the least common multiple of 20 and 36?

....

....

....

....

8 **a)** What is the highest common factor of 64 and 100?

....

....

....

....

b) What is the least common multiple of 64 and 100?

....

....

....

....

9 **Kate, Tessa and Pat are clapping out a rhythm. Kate claps every 3 beats. Tessa claps every 5 beats. Pat claps every 9 beats. They all start clapping at the same time. How many beats is it before they all clap at the same time again?**

....

10 **a)** The highest common factor of two numbers is 4. The least common multiple of the same two numbers is 60. What are the two numbers?

....

....

b) The highest common factor of three numbers is 15. The least common multiple of the same three numbers is 90. What are the three numbers?

....

....

---

11 **Here are ten numbers:**

9, 14, 25, 29, 41, 50, 61, 70, 84, 100

a) Which three numbers are **i)** factors of 200, **ii)** multiples of 25, **iii)** multiples of 7, **iv)** prime numbers?
b) Which of the above numbers has the reciprocal 0.02?

12 **What is the reciprocal of a)** 100, **b)** $\frac{1}{100}$, **c)** 0.01, **d)** $\frac{99}{100}$?

13 **Express the following numbers in prime factor form: a)** 30, **b)** 100, **c)** 2 048

14 **What is the highest common factor and least common multiple of...**
a) 15 and 18, **b)** 40 and 58, **c)** 15, 18 and 24?

Integers 1 & 2

1 a) Put the following integers into ascending order (lowest to highest):

14, -3, -1, 5, 12, -7, -11, 2

....

b) Put the following integers into descending order (highest to lowest):

-230, 467, 165, -62, -162, 70, -320, 8

....

2 Complete the following boxes:

a) i) $1 - 3 + \boxed{} = 6$ **ii)** $6 + \boxed{} = 2$ **iii)** $-6 + \boxed{} = -11$

    iv) $-4 - \boxed{} = -9$ **v)** $4 - \boxed{} = -4$ **vi)** $-3 - \boxed{} = 5$

    vii) $-6 \times \boxed{} = 12$ **viii)** $5 \times \boxed{} = -20$ **ix)** $-6 \times \boxed{} = 6$

    x) $-12 \div \boxed{} = -2$ **xi)** $36 \div \boxed{} = -9$ **xii)** $-45 \div \boxed{} = 9$

b) i) $-4 - 6 + \boxed{} = 2$ **ii)** $6 - \boxed{} - 3 = 11$ **iii)** $-8 - 3 - \boxed{} = 5$

    iv) $\boxed{} + 2 - 5 = -9$ **v)** $14 - 1 + \boxed{} = -15$ **vi)** $4 - 11 + \boxed{} = -5$

c) i) $\dfrac{-6 + \boxed{}}{-3} = 7$ **ii)** $\dfrac{-6 + 2 - \boxed{}}{-5} = 4$ **iii)** $\dfrac{\boxed{} - 6 - 3}{-1} = 4$

    iv) $\dfrac{-3 \times -5 \times \boxed{}}{-6} = 10$ **v)** $\dfrac{9 \times \boxed{} \times -2}{4 - 6} = 9$

d) i) $\boxed{} + \boxed{} = -4$ **ii)** $\boxed{} - \boxed{} = -3$ **iii)** $\boxed{} \times \boxed{} = -18$

    iv) $\boxed{} \div \boxed{} = -10$ **v)** $\boxed{} \times -5 \times \boxed{} = 30$

3 Complete the following boxes by inserting =, +, –, x or ÷ to connect the numbers:

a) $6 \boxed{} 9 \boxed{} -3$ **b)** $2 \boxed{} 3 \boxed{} -7 \boxed{} 12$

c) $9 \boxed{} 1 \boxed{} -3 \boxed{} -3$ **d)** $-50 \boxed{} 10 \boxed{} 5 \boxed{} 0$

e) $6 \boxed{} -3 \boxed{} 10 \boxed{} 19 \boxed{} 1$

f) $10 \boxed{} -2 \boxed{} 6 \boxed{} 2 \boxed{} 0$

4 The following table shows the highest temperatures (in °C) for eight places on a particular day:

Place	Athens	Berlin	Cairo	Cardiff	London	Madrid	Moscow	New York
Temperature	15	-2	25	2	6	13	-6	18

a) What is the difference in temperature between the following places:

i) Athens and Berlin?...

ii) Cairo and Moscow? ....

iii) Berlin and Moscow?..

b) The next day the temperature in Cardiff had fallen by 2°C and the temperature in Moscow had fallen by 5°C. What was the difference between Cardiff and Moscow on that day?

....

5 Below is part of a bank statement:

LONSDALE BUILDING SOCIETY

Date	Description	Deposit	Withdrawal	Balance
11/12/03				£226.30
12/12/03	The Toy Shop		-£49.99	£176.31
13/12/03	Gas Bill		-£21.03	£155.28
13/12/03	Cheque	£25.00		£180.28
16/12/03	La Trattoria		-£32.98	[ ]
19/12/03	Rent		[ ]	-£112.70

a) What was the balance on 16/12/03 after the withdrawal of £32.98?

....

b) On 19/12/03 there was a withdrawal to pay for rent. How much was the withdrawal?

....

6 Put the following integers into ascending order:

3, -3, -11, 0, 4, 19, -36, 74, -1, 100

7 Complete the following:

a) 6 – 8 =   b) -4 – 4 =   c) -1 – 1 + 2 =   d) -5 x -6 x 10 =   e) -5 x 3 x 6 =   f) -15 ÷ 3 x -4 =   g) 100 ÷ 4 x -1 =

8 Fill in the following boxes:

a) [ ] – 3 = 12 b) -8 – [ ] = 3 c) -6 + [ ] – 2 = 11 d) -14 + 20 + [ ] = -10 e) [ ] + 4 – 8 = -15

Upper and Lower Bounds

1 a) Some ribbon is measured as 7.4cm to the nearest mm. What are the upper and lower bounds of the length of the ribbon?

....

b) Kevin cut off 3.2cm of ribbon. Find the greatest and shortest lengths of ribbon left.

....

....

2 The weight of a BMW car is given as 1 900kg to the nearest 100kg. Find the difference between the greatest and least possible weight of this car as a percentage of the given weight.

....

....

3 A vending machine dispenses 125ml of black tea into cups with a capacity of 166ml. These values are accurate to 3 significant figures.

Milk is supplied in small cartons which hold 19ml, accurate to the nearest ml.

Cassie likes milky tea and always puts two cartons of milk in her tea.

Will Cassie's cup ever overflow?

Show all your working.

....

....

....

....

....

....

....

....

....

4 A crane has a cable with a breaking strain of 6 200kg measured to 2 significant figures. It is used to lift crates which weigh 110kg to the nearest 10kg. What is the greatest number of crates that can be lifted at one time so that the cable does not break?

5 A car travels at an average speed of 37.6 miles per hour over a distance of 53.2 miles. Both measurements are correct to 1 d.p. Calculate the range of possible values for the time taken.

Estimating and Checking

1 **a) i)** Work out 106 x 53 using a calculator ....

    ii) Without using a calculator check your answer by estimation.

....

  b) i) Work out 3.8 x 15.2 using a calculator ....

  ii) Without using a calculator check your answer by estimation.

....

  c) i) Work out $\dfrac{49.6 \times 5.8}{(9.98)^2}$ using a calculator ....

  ii) Without using a calculator check your answer by estimation.

....

  d) i) Work out 384 726 x 0.00071 using a calculator ....

  ii) Without using a calculator check your answer by estimation.

....

2 **John and Donna collect and keep all their loose change. The table below shows how much they collected for three successive months.**

MONTH	JOHN	DONNA
JUNE	£7.36	£9.10
JULY	£8.90	£16.58
AUGUST	£13.47	£4.52

a) John calculates that he collected £29.73 altogether.

i) Check by estimation whether this is likely to be correct.

....

ii) Check John's calculation for accuracy.

....

....

b) Donna calculates that she collected £31.20 altogether.

i) Check by estimation whether this is likely to be correct.

....

ii) Check Donna's calculation for accuracy.

....

....

3 **Check the following calculations by estimation and then for accuracy. Finish by making any necessary corrections.**
  a) 13 + 29 + 43 = 82 **b)** 9.06 + 11.58 + 7.23 + 13.86 = 41.73
  c) (3 x 6.25) + 92 − 10 = 101.75 **d)** (4.7 x 6.3) + (0.8 x 9.5) = 40.21

4 **Use approximations to estimate the value of ...** $\dfrac{312 \times 4.01}{0.198}$

Powers 1 & 2

1 **Work out the value of...**

a) 2^3 ....

b) 3^2 ....

c) 4^3 ....

d) 10^3 ....

e) 3^4 ....

f) 1^5 ....

2 **Here are ten numbers:**

$$10 \quad 18 \quad 25 \quad 27 \quad 45 \quad 64 \quad 80 \quad 125 \quad 133 \quad 196$$

a) Which three numbers are square numbers? ....

b) Which three numbers are cube numbers? ....

c) Which one of these numbers is a square number and a cube number? ....

d) Which of the above numbers is equal to $10^2 - 6^2$? ....

e) Which of the above numbers is equal to $4^3 + 2^4$? ....

3 **Work out the value of...**

a) $(-3)^2$ ....

b) $(-3)^3$ ....

c) $(-5)^2$ ....

d) $(-5)^3$ ....

e) $(-1)^2$ ....

f) $(-1)^3$ ....

4 **Find the value of ...**

a) $2^3 \times 2^2$ ....

b) $3^2 \times 3^1$ ....

c) $4^3 \times 4^2 \times 4^1$ ....

d) $2^3 \div 2^2$ ....

e) $10^4 \div 10^2$ ....

f) $6^4 \div 6^0$ ....

g) $(2^2)^2$ ....

h) $(4^3)^2$ ....

i) $(10^2)^3$ ....

j) $(2^2 \times 2^3)^2$ ....

k) $\dfrac{10^2 - 6^2}{4^3}$ ....

l) $\dfrac{4^3 + 2^6}{8^2}$ ....

m) $\dfrac{(4^1)^3}{8^2}$ ....

n) $\dfrac{2^2 \times 2^1 \times 2^4}{4^3}$ ....

5 **Work out the value of...**

a) $27^{\frac{2}{3}}$ ....

b) $64^{\frac{2}{3}}$ ....

c) 16 ....

d) $100\,000^{\frac{4}{5}}$ ....

e) $1\,024^{\frac{2}{5}}$ ....

f) 1 ....

6 **Work out the value of...**

a) 4^4 b) 4^1 c) $4^4 \times 4^1$ d) $4^3 \times 5^2$ e) $8^0 + 3^3$ f) $6^2 - 3^2$ g) $\dfrac{8^2}{2^5}$ h) $\dfrac{3^3 - 7^1}{2^2}$ i) $\dfrac{10^2 + 3^3 + 5^0}{8^2}$

7 a) What is $3^3 \times 9^2$ as a single power of 3? b) What is $5^2 - 3^2$ as a single power of 2? c) What is $8^2 \times 2^4$ as a single power of 4?

8 **Simplify $6^{-2} \times 144^{0.5}$**

1 **Work out the value of...**

a) $\sqrt{25}$ .... **b)** $36^{\frac{1}{2}}$ .... **c)** $\sqrt{144}$ ....

d) $196^{\frac{1}{2}}$ .... **e)** $64^{\frac{1}{3}}$ .... **f)** $\sqrt[3]{1}$ ....

g) $8^{\frac{1}{3}}$ .... **h)** $\sqrt[3]{1000}$ .... **i)** $27^{\frac{1}{3}}$ ....

2 **a)** You are given that $\sqrt{24} + \sqrt{54} = a\sqrt{6}$ where 'a' is an integer. Find the value of 'a'.

....

....

b) Find the value of $(p + q)^2$ when $p = \sqrt{3}$ and $q = \sqrt{12}$.

....

....

....

3 **Work out the value of...**

a) $(\sqrt{4})^2$ .... **b)** $(\sqrt[3]{8})^2$ .... **c)** $\sqrt{4^2 \times 25}$ ....

d) $100^{\frac{1}{2}} \times \sqrt[3]{27}$ .... **e)** $64^{\frac{1}{2}} \times \sqrt[3]{64}$ .... **f)** $16^{\frac{3}{2}}$ ....

4 **a)** What is $\sqrt{4} \times 8$ as a single power of 4? ....

b) What is $\sqrt[3]{27} \times 3$ as a single power of 3? ....

c) What is $\sqrt[3]{64} \times 16^{\frac{1}{2}}$ as a single power of 2? ....

d) What is $\sqrt{9} \times 1^3 \times \sqrt{144}$ as a single power of 6? ....

5 **Simplify the following surds:**

a) $\sqrt{27}$ .... **b)** $\sqrt{50}$ ....

c) $\sqrt{54}$ .... **d)** $\sqrt{90}$ ....

e) $\dfrac{\sqrt{15}}{\sqrt{3}}$ .... **f)** $(5 - \sqrt{7})^2$ ....

6 **a)** Rationalise the denominator of $\dfrac{4}{\sqrt{7}}$.

b) Rationalise the denominator of $\dfrac{4 + \sqrt{5}}{\sqrt{5}}$.

7 **Work out the value of ...**
a) $169^{\frac{1}{2}}$ **b)** $\sqrt[3]{125}$ **c)** $\sqrt{81}$ **d)** $125^{\frac{1}{3}}$ **e)** $225^{\frac{1}{2}}$

8 **Find the value of ...**
a) $(\sqrt{9})^3$ **b)** $(\sqrt[3]{8})^2$ **c)** $\sqrt[3]{6^2 + 28}$ **d)** 4 **e)** 64

9 **Simplify the following surds:**
a) $\sqrt{200}$ **b)** $\sqrt{80}$ **c)** $\sqrt{63}$

10 **Without using a calculator, find the exact value of x.**

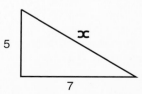

Standard Form

1 **Write the following examples of standard form as ordinary numbers:**

a) 6.32×10^1 ....

b) 7.467×10^3 ....

c) 3×10^{-2} ....

d) 2.3×10^{-3} ....

e) 4.21×10^{-4} ....

f) 6.324×10^{-2} ....

2 **Write the following numbers in standard form:**

a) 413 256 ....

b) 496.3 ....

c) 0.032 ....

d) 0.47 ....

e) 0.000631 ....

f) 0.1 ....

3 **a)** The star Alpha Centauri is approximately 40 653 000 000 000km from the earth. Write this number in standard form to 3 significant figures.

....

b) Light travels at approximately 3 298 000km per second. There are 86 400 seconds in a day. How many days will light take to reach the earth from Alpha Centauri? Give your answer to an appropriate degree of accuracy.

....

....

4 **Calculate the following. Give your answers in standard form.**

a) $9.23 \times 10^2 + 4.71 \times 10^3$ ....

b) $7.15 \times 10^5 - 9.68 \times 10^4$ ....

c) $2.34 \times 10^4 \times 3.6 \times 10^7$ ....

d) $5.5 \times 10^7 \div 1.1 \times 10^9$ ....

5 In 1901 the population of England and Wales was 3.26×10^7. If the area of England and Wales is 151 000km^2 (to the nearest thousand), calculate what the population per square kilometre was in 1901. Give your answer to 2 significant figures.

6 In one minute light will travel a distance of approximately 1.8×10^{10} metres.
a) How far will light travel in 1 hour? Give your answer in standard form.
b) How far will light travel in 1 year? Give your answer in standard form.
c) The sun is approximately 1.44×10^{11} metres away. How long does it take light to travel from the sun to the earth?
d) A light year is the distance travelled by light in one earth year. Our nearest star, after the sun, is 4.3 light years away. How far away is this star in metres? Give your answer in standard form.

7 Here are 5 numbers written in standard form: 3.2×10^6 1.05×10^7 4.91×10^0 9.6×10^{-3} 5.2×10^{-1}
a) Write down **i)** the largest number.
            ii) the smallest number.
b) Write down 9.6×10^{-3} as an ordinary number.
c) Work out $3.2 \times 10^6 \div 0.1$ giving your answer in standard form.

Fractions 1

1 Here are eight fractions:

$$\frac{35}{50}, \frac{16}{40}, \frac{60}{90}, \frac{28}{40}, \frac{30}{40}, \frac{40}{100}, \frac{84}{120}, \frac{10}{25}$$

a) Which three fractions are equivalent to $\frac{2}{5}$? ....

b) Which three fractions are equivalent to $\frac{7}{10}$? ....

2 Express the following fractions in their simplest form:

a) $\frac{27}{30}$ .... **b)** $\frac{42}{6}$ .... **c)** $\frac{84}{105}$ .... **d)** $\frac{108}{184}$ ....

3 **a)** Arrange the following fractions in ascending (lowest to highest) order:

$$\frac{5}{6}, \frac{3}{5}, \frac{11}{15}, \frac{2}{3}, \frac{1}{2}$$

....

b) Arrange the following fractions in descending (highest to lowest) order:

$$\frac{9}{40}, \frac{3}{5}, \frac{5}{8}, \frac{9}{10}, \frac{1}{4}$$

....

4 Write down two fractions that are greater than $\frac{7}{10}$ but less than $\frac{5}{6}$.

....

5 **a)** Write the following improper fractions as mixed numbers:

i) $\frac{11}{5}$ .... **ii)** $\frac{13}{6}$ .... **iii)** $\frac{24}{5}$ .... **iv)** $\frac{32}{3}$ ....

b) Write the following mixed numbers as improper fractions:

i) $3\frac{1}{3}$ .... **ii)** $5\frac{1}{4}$ .... **iii)** $11\frac{3}{5}$ .... **iv)** $20\frac{1}{20}$ ....

6 Write down three fractions that are equivalent to each of the following:
a) $\frac{2}{3}$ **b)** $\frac{4}{7}$ **c)** $\frac{9}{11}$

7 Express the following fractions in their simplest form and then arrange them into ascending order:
$$\frac{28}{35}, \frac{38}{40}, \frac{75}{100}, \frac{42}{84}, \frac{99}{110}$$

8 Write down three fractions that are greater than $\frac{4}{5}$ but less than $\frac{9}{10}$.

Fractions 2

1 Solve the following additions and subtractions without using a calculator. Show all your working and give your answers in their simplest form.

a) $\dfrac{3}{4} + \dfrac{2}{3}$

b) $\dfrac{2}{9} + \dfrac{7}{8}$

c) $4\dfrac{1}{2} + 2\dfrac{9}{10}$

d) $7\dfrac{5}{8} + 4\dfrac{1}{3}$

e) $\dfrac{9}{10} - \dfrac{1}{2}$

f) $\dfrac{13}{15} - \dfrac{2}{3}$

g) $4\dfrac{4}{5} - 1\dfrac{3}{8}$

h) $9\dfrac{1}{6} - 4\dfrac{3}{5}$

2 At a football match the crowd is made up as follows:

$\dfrac{5}{12}$ of the crowd are over 40 years old, $\dfrac{1}{4}$ of the crowd is between 20 years old and 40 years old, and the remainder of the crowd is less than 20 years old.

What fraction of the crowd is less than 20 years old? Give your answer in its simplest form.

....

....

....

....

3 Solve the following multiplications and divisions without using a calculator. Show all your working and give your answers in their simplest form.

a) $\dfrac{1}{4} \times \dfrac{2}{5}$

b) $\dfrac{9}{10} \times \dfrac{2}{7}$

c) $\dfrac{3}{4} \div \dfrac{9}{10}$

d) $\dfrac{7}{8} \div \dfrac{7}{12}$

e) $3\dfrac{1}{2} \times 1\dfrac{3}{5}$

f) $3\dfrac{1}{4} \times 1\dfrac{5}{7}$

g) $4\dfrac{1}{2} \div 2\dfrac{2}{3}$

h) $1\dfrac{1}{2} \div 2\dfrac{1}{4}$

i) $\dfrac{8}{9} \times 4$

j) $\dfrac{7}{10} \div 3$

4 Solve the following without using a calculator. Show all your working.

a) $\dfrac{7}{10} + \dfrac{5}{8}$ b) $2\dfrac{1}{3} + 4\dfrac{3}{8}$ c) $\dfrac{9}{10} - \dfrac{2}{3}$ d) $4\dfrac{1}{2} - 3\dfrac{7}{10}$ e) $\dfrac{2}{5} \times \dfrac{7}{10}$ f) $\dfrac{13}{15} \div \dfrac{4}{5}$

g) $3\dfrac{1}{4} \times 1\dfrac{2}{3}$ h) $4\dfrac{1}{5} \div 3\dfrac{1}{2}$ i) $4\dfrac{1}{2} \times 5$ j) $2\dfrac{1}{3} \div 6$

Calculations Involving Fractions

1 James wants to buy a CD player costing £240.

As a deposit he pays $\frac{1}{8}$ of the cost. How much deposit did James pay?

....

....

2 Mary buys a new car costing £13 000.

As a deposit she pays $\frac{2}{5}$ of the cost. The remainder she pays monthly over a period of 4 years.

a) How much deposit does Mary pay?

....

....

b) What is her monthly repayment?

....

....

c) At the end of the 4 years Mary decides to sell her car. It is now worth £7150. Express its value now, after 4 years, as a fraction of its value when new. Give your answer in its simplest form.

....

....

3 A shop holds a sale where all items are reduced by $\frac{1}{6}$.

a) Calculate the sale price of an item which cost £93.60 before the sale.

....

....

....

b) The sale price of another item is £121.50. Calculate its price before it was reduced.

....

....

....

4 A football match lasts $1\frac{1}{2}$ hours. During the match the ball is out of play for a total of 15 minutes. Express the total length of time that the ball is in play as a fraction of the time that the match lasts. Give your answer in its simplest form.

5 In a sale, a washing machine has its original price reduced by $\frac{1}{2}$. The following week the sale price is further reduced by $\frac{1}{4}$.

a) If the washing machine originally cost £600, calculate its sale price after **i)** the first reduction, **ii)** the second reduction.
b) If the washing machine costs £150 after both reductions what was its original price?

6 Express 40 seconds as a fraction of 1 hour.

Decimals 1 & 2

1 Complete the following table (the first row has been done for you).

	Place Value of Digits							Decimal Number
	100 Hundreds	**10** Tens	**1** Units	DECIMAL POINT	$\frac{1}{10}$ Tenths	$\frac{1}{100}$ Hundredths	$\frac{1}{1000}$ Thousandths	
			3	•	4	2		3.42
a)	1	0	2		5			
b)		1	3		4	7	1	
c)								8.407
d)		9	0		0	3	1	
e)								423.008

2 Use a calculator to write the following fractions as either recurring or terminating decimals. If the decimal is recurring, place a dot (•) over the digit or digits that repeat continuously.

a) $\frac{2}{3}$ .... b) $\frac{2}{5}$ .... c) $\frac{1}{11}$ .... d) $\frac{7}{9}$ ....

3 Arrange the following decimals in ascending order of value:

$$6.3, \ 0.36, \ 3.6, \ 0.306, \ 0.63$$

....

4 Convert the following recurring decimals into fractions:

a) $0.\overset{\bullet\bullet}{63}$ b) $0.\overset{\bullet\quad\bullet}{432}$

....

....

....

....

5 Write the following fractions as decimals. For each recurring decimal, place a dot (·) over the digit or digits that repeat continuously.

a) $\frac{3}{8}$ b) $\frac{2}{9}$ c) $\frac{1}{30}$ d) $\frac{22}{25}$ e) $\frac{4}{15}$

6 Arrange the following decimals in descending (highest to lowest) order:
14.32, 1.432, 143.2, 13.42, 14.23, 1.342

7 Mrs Green goes shopping. She buys four tins of baked beans at 37p each, three tins of spaghetti at 29p each and two boxes of cornflakes at £1.37 each. She pays for her goods with a £10 note. How much change does she receive?

8 a) Prove that $0.\overset{\bullet\bullet}{34} = \frac{34}{99}$ b) Hence or otherwise, express $0.1\overset{\bullet\bullet}{34}$ as a fraction.

Multiplication of Decimals

1 **Solve the following without using a calculator. Where possible show all your working.**

    a) 4.7 x 10   **b)** 13.246 x 10   **c)** 0.00146 x 100   **d)** 136.3 x 1 000

    ....

    e) 7.56 x 13   **f)** 4.72 x 2.3

    g) 16.56 x 17.3   **h)** 4.713 x 1.56

2 **If 27 x 36 = 972 write down, without making any further calculations, the value of...**

    a) 2.7 x 36   ....   **b)** 27 x 0.36   ....   **c)** 2.7 x 3.6   ....

    d) 0.027 x 36   ....   **e)** 0.27 x 0.36   ....

3 **If 231 x 847 = 195 657 write down, without making any further calculations, the value of...**

    a) 0.231 x 847   ....   **b)** 231 x 84 700   ....

    c) 0.231 x 847 000   ....   **d)** 2 310 x 8.47   ....

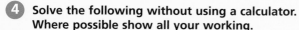

4 **Solve the following without using a calculator.**
Where possible show all your working.
    a) 15.67 x 10   **b)** 0.0101 x 100   **c)** 3.4671 x 1000   **d)** 2.32 x 11
    e) 4.67 x 1.8   **f)** 146.2 x 2.45   **g)** 13.33 x 0.23   **h)** 9.4 x 0.003

5 **If 3.52 x 4.7 = 16.544 write down, without making any further**
calculations, the value of...
    a) 352 x 47   **b)** 3.52 x 47   **c)** 0.352 x 4.7   **d)** 3.52 x 0.047

6 **A school holds a raffle. The three prizes cost £24.65, £17.99 and**
£9.89. 130 tickets were sold at £1.25 each.
How much profit did the school make from the raffle?

7 **Jim is going to hire a cement mixer. The cost is £24.50 for the**
first day and £3.75 for each extra day. Jim wants to hire it for 7
days. How much will it cost him in total?

8 **A shirt costs £24.95. How much is this in euros if £1 = €1.6?**

£24.95

Division of Decimals

1 Solve the following without using a calculator. Where possible show all your working.

a) 16.3 ÷ 10

b) 0.347 ÷ 10

c) 14 632.4 ÷ 100

d) 1.2467 ÷ 1 000

e) 37.6 ÷ 8

f) 41.04 ÷ 1.2

g) 1 141.72 ÷ 0.23

h) 549.6 ÷ 1.2

2 If 72.8 ÷ 56 = 1.3 write down, without making any further calculations, the value of...

a) 72.8 ÷ 5.6

b) 7.28 ÷ 56

c) 72.8 ÷ 0.56

d) 0.728 ÷ 56

e) 728 ÷ 56

3 If 27 x 34 = 918 write down, without making any further calculations, the value of...

a) 918 ÷ 27

b) 918 ÷ 3.4

c) 91.8 ÷ 27

d) 9.18 ÷ 3.4

e) 91.8 ÷ 340

4 Solve the following without using a calculator. Where possible show all your working.
a) 7.162 ÷ 10   b) 0.0034 ÷ 100   c) 473.1 ÷ 1 000   d) 707.4 ÷ 9   e) 24.64 ÷ 1.4   f) 0.08788 ÷ 0.0013

5 If 58.82 ÷ 3.4 = 17.3 write down, without making any further calculations, the value of...
a) 58.82 ÷ 0.34   b) 5 882 ÷ 0.34   c) 58.82 ÷ 17.3   d) 3.4 x 17.3

6 A school holds a raffle. The three prizes cost £9.49, £14.99 and £19.99. Tickets cost 75p each. What is the minimum number of tickets that need to be sold for the school to make a profit?

7 Jean is going to hire a wallpaper stripper. The cost is £8.50 for the first day and £1.25 for each extra day. When she returns the wallpaper stripper the total hire charge is £24.75. For how many days did she hire the wallpaper stripper?

Percentages 1

1 Calculate the following amounts:

a) 20% of 60p

b) 30% of 6.5km

....

....

....

....

2 Express ...

a) £18 as a percentage of £90

b) 42cm as a percentage of 8.4m

....

....

....

....

3 Alan has kept a record of his height and weight from when he was age 10 and age 16.

Age 10	1.2m tall	40kg weight
Age 16	1.74m tall	64kg weight

a) i) Calculate the increase in his height from age 10 to age 16 ....

ii) Express this increase as a percentage of his height at age 10.

....

....

b) i) Calculate the increase in his weight from age 10 to age 16 ....

ii) Express this increase as a percentage of his weight at age 10.

....

....

4 A train ticket costs £17.60 when bought on the day of travel. If the same ticket is bought in advance it costs £15.40. Express the saving you make when you buy the ticket in advance as a percentage of the full ticket price when bought on the day of travel.

....

....

....

5 Calculate the following amounts:
a) 45% of £2.60 **b)** 80% of 6.4kg **c)** 5% of £10.40.

6 **a)** Express 46cm as a percentage of 69cm **b)** Express 200m as a percentage of 200km
c) Express 550g as a percentage of 2kg

7 A tin of tomato soup weighs 420g. Special tins weigh 546g. Calculate the increase in the weight of a special tin as a percentage of the weight of a normal tin.

8 A brand new car bought in the UK costs £18 000. The same car bought abroad costs £14 850. Calculate the decrease in the price when the car is bought abroad as a percentage of its price in the UK.

Percentages 2

1 A brand new car costs £15 000. It is estimated that it will depreciate in value by 23% during the first year. What will the value of the car be at the end of the first year?

....

....

2 The average attendance at a football club over a season was 32 500. In the next season there was a 6% increase in the average attendance. What was the average attendance for that season?

....

....

3 Mr and Mrs Smith bought a house for £120 000. Each year since the value of the property has appreciated by 10%.

a) Calculate the value of the house two years after they bought it.

....

....

b) The value of the house after two years can be found by multiplying the original cost by a single number. What is this single number as a decimal?

....

4 Jim buys a new motorbike for £10 000.

a) If the value of the motorbike decreases by 20% each year, calculate the value of the motorbike after three years.

....

....

b) The value of Jim's bike after three years can be found by multiplying the original cost by a single number. What is this single number as a decimal?

....

5 An electrical shop has a sale. All items are reduced by 20%. The following week the shop takes 10% off its sale prices. Pat wants to buy a fridge that was priced at £100 before the sale. She reckons that she will save 30% of this price and that the fridge will now cost her £70. Is she correct? Explain why.

6 Bob weighs 120kg on January 1. Over the first six months of the year his weight increases by 5%. Over the next six months his weight decreases by 10%.
a) What is his weight at the end of the year?
b) Bob's weight at the end of the year can be found by multiplying his weight on January 1 by a single number. What is this single number as a decimal?

Percentages 3

1 Phil has been told by his mum that he needs to spend 1 hour a day doing his homework, an increase of 50%. How long did Phil originally spend doing his homework each day?

....

....

....

2 An electrical shop has a sale. All items are reduced by 15%. A tumble drier has a sale price of £122.40. What was the price of the tumble drier before the sale?

....

....

....

3 A man buys an antique clock. He later sells it for £5 040, an increase of 12% on the price he paid for it. How much did the clock cost him?

....

....

....

....

4 Dave is a long distance lorry driver. On Tuesday he drives 253km. This is a 15% increase on the distance he drove the previous day. How far did he drive on Monday?

....

....

....

5 Jean has her house valued. It is worth £84 000. This is a 40% increase on the price she originally paid for it. How much did Jean pay for her house?

....

....

....

6 A clothes shop has a sale. All prices are reduced by 30%. The sale price of a dress is £86.80. What was the original price of the dress?

7 Mrs Smith buys some shares. In twelve months their value has increased by 15% to £3 680. How much did she pay for the shares?

8 Mr Jones collects stamps. After two years he has increased the number of stamps in his collection by 120% to 660. How many stamps did he have in his collection two years ago?

Converting Between Systems

1 Complete the following table. The first row has been done for you.

	Fraction (simplest form)	Decimal	Percentage
	$\frac{1}{2}$	0.5	50%
a)	$\frac{3}{10}$		
b)		0.45	
c)			37.5%
d)	$\frac{2}{3}$		
e)		0.125	
f)			84%
g)	$1\frac{4}{5}$		
h)		4.6	
i)			225%

2 $\frac{3}{5}$ of the CDs in Peter's collection are pop music. Is this more or less than 55% of his collection?

Explain your answer.

....

....

3 **a)** Write the following fractions and percentages as decimals:

i) $\frac{2}{5}$ .... **ii)** 35% .... **iii)** $\frac{1}{3}$ .... **iv)** 44% ....

b) Write these numbers in ascending order:

$$44\%, \quad \frac{2}{5}, \quad 35\%, \quad 0.42, \quad \frac{1}{3}, \quad 0.25$$

....

....

4 **a)** Write the following as decimals: **i)** $\frac{4}{5}$ **ii)** 90% **iii)** $\frac{17}{20}$ **iv)** 85%

b) Write the following numbers in descending order: $\frac{19}{20}$, 0.75, 90%, 0.92, $\frac{4}{5}$, 85%

5 **a)** Write the following as percentages: **i)** 0.62 **ii)** $\frac{3}{5}$ **iii)** 0.56 **iv)** $\frac{29}{50}$

b) Write the following numbers in ascending order: 61%, $\frac{3}{5}$, 0.56, 0.62, $\frac{29}{50}$, 65%

Everyday Maths 1 & 2

1 a) Alma buys a washing machine. The price is £380 + VAT at 17.5%.

How much does the washing machine cost in total?

....

....

b) The total cost of a home stereo system is £517 including VAT at 17.5%.

What is the price of the home stereo system before VAT?

....

....

2 Mr Smith wants to invest £20 000 for two years. He has two options:

SIMPLE INTEREST AT 5% OR COMPOUND INTEREST AT 4.8%

a) Which option will make him the most money? Show all your working.

....

....

....

b) Which option will make him the most money after five years?
Show all your working.

....

....

....

....

....

....

....

3 Peter wants to buy a car. There are two payment options:

Cash price £8 000 or hire purchase of 30% deposit + 24 monthly payments of £255

a) What is the deposit required for hire purchase?

....

b) Calculate the percentage increase if Peter pays for the car by hire purchase compared to buying the
car at the cash price.

....

....

....

Everyday Maths 1 & 2 (cont)

4 Mr Spark receives an electricity bill. Complete the bill by filling in the gaps.

Meter Reading				
Present	Previous	Units Used	Pence per unit	Amount (£)
32467	30277	i)	8p	ii) ....
			Quarterly charge	9.60
		Total charged this quarter excluding VAT		iii) ....
		VAT at 5%		iv) ....
		Total payable		v) ....

5 Use the timetable alongside to answer the following questions:

a) Grace wants to arrive in London before midday. What is the latest train she can catch from Millford station to get there in time and how long will her train journey take?

....

....

b) Simon needs to get to Woking by 11.15am because he has a job interview. What is the time of the last train he can catch from Farncombe?

....

c) What percentage of trains departing from Woking station take less than 30 minutes to arrive at London Waterloo?

....

....

Petersfield, Millford, Farncombe, Woking to London Waterloo

Mondays to Fridays

	AN	NW	AN	AN	AN
Petersfield	0752	0811	0833	0901	0928
Liphook	—	—	—	—	—
Haslemere	—	—	—	—	—
Witley	—	—	—	—	—
Millford (Surrey)	0806	0829	0845	0917	0941
Godalming	—	—	—	—	—
Farncombe	0822	0850	0900	0937	0959
Guildford	—	—	—	—	—
Reading	—	—	—	—	—
Woking	0830	0900	0907	0947	1007
Heathrow Airport (T1)	—	—	—	—	—
Clapham Junction	—	—	—	—	—
London Waterloo	0903	0932	0939	1018	1036

Mondays to Fridays

	AN	NW	AN	AN	AN
Petersfield	0949	0956	1019	1049	1055
Liphook	—	—	—	—	—
Haslemere	—	—	—	—	—
Witley	—	—	—	—	—
Millford (Surrey)	1002	1011	1032	1102	1114
Godalming	—	—	—	—	—
Farncombe	1017	1032	1047	1117	1132
Guildford	—	—	—	—	—
Reading	—	—	—	—	—
Woking	1026	1043	1059	1128	1142
Heathrow Airport (T1)	—	—	—	—	—
Clapham Junction	—	—	—	—	—
London Waterloo	1052	1111	1125	1155	1211

6 What is the total cost of a vacuum cleaner if the price is £180 + VAT at 17.5%?

7 Mr Walker wants to invest £20 000 for 3 years. He can either invest it at 6% simple interest or 5.5% compound interest. Which option will make him the most money? Show all your working.

8 Mr Brum wants to buy a car costing £6 000. He buys it on hire purchase paying £124 a month for 3 years. His total repayment is £6 264. What deposit did he pay as a percentage of the car's value?

9 Mr Plug receives an electricity bill. The cost per unit is 8p and the quarterly charge is £9.60. It says on his bill that the total payable for this quarter excluding VAT is £80.24. How many units has he used this quarter?

10 £3 200 is invested at 4.8% compound interest per annum. How many years will it take for the investment to exceed £4 000?

Ratio and Proportion 1

1 $\frac{3}{7}$ of the teachers at a school are male.

    a) What is the ratio of male teachers to female teachers? ....

    b) Express your answer to part a) in the form 1:n ....

2 A large tin of baked beans costs 36p and weighs 450g. A small tin of baked beans costs 22p and weighs 250g.

    a) Calculate the ratio of the weight of the two tins ....

    b) Calculate the ratio of the cost of the two tins ....

    c) Which tin represents the best value for money? Explain your choice.

    ....

3 £5 000 is shared between three women in the ratio of their ages. Their combined age is 120 years. If Susan gets £2 500, Janet gets £1 500 and Polly gets the remainder, what are their ages?

    ....

    ....

    ....

4 In a maths class there are 30 pupils on the register and the ratio of girls to boys is 3:2. If 4 girls and 2 boys are absent from the class what does the ratio of girls to boys become?

    ....

    ....

    ....

    ....

5 A builder makes concrete by mixing cement, gravel, sand and water in the ratio 2:8:5:3 by weight. How many kilograms of sand, to the nearest kg, does he need to make 10 000kg of concrete?

    ....

    ....

    ....

    ....

    ....

6 100ml of semi-skimmed milk contains 4.8g carbohydrates and 1.8g fat.
    a) What is the ratio of carbohydrates to fat? **b)** Express your answer to part a) in the form 1:n.

7 Mr Thorpe inherits £15 000. He divides the money between his four children, Lucy, Paul, John and Sarah, in the ratio 6:7:8:9 respectively. How much do they each receive?

8 450 tickets were sold for a raffle at 20p each. The ratio of the cost of prizes to profit made is 5:13. How much profit did the raffle make?

9 The angles of a quadrilateral are in the ratio 2:3:5:8. What is the size of the largest angle?

10 A large packet of washing powder weighs 2.5kg and costs £5.60. How much should a 750g packet of washing powder cost if it represents the same value as the large packet?

Ratio and Proportion 2

1 **y is directly proportional to x^2 and y is equal to 16 when x is equal to 8.**

    a) What is the value of y when x is equal to 12?

    b) What is the value of x when y is equal to 100?

....

....

....

....

....

2 **y is inversely proportional to x^2 and y is equal to 4 when x is equal to 3.**

    a) What is the value of y when x is equal to 6?

    b) What is the value of x when y is equal to 12?
        Leave your answer in surd form.

....

....

....

....

....

3 **The volume, V, of a sphere is directly proportional to the cube of its radius, r. If a sphere has a volume of 33.6cm³ when its radius is 2cm, calculate the radius of a sphere of volume 14.175cm³.**

....

....

....

....

....

....

4 **The pressure, P, exerted by a constant force is inversely proportional to the area, A, over which the force acts. If the pressure exerted is 15N/cm² when the area is 12cm², calculate the pressure exerted when the area is 9cm².**

....

....

....

....

....

....

5 **a is directly proportional to bc and a is equal to 120 when b is equal to 6 and c is equal to 4.**
    a) Calculate the value of a when b = 10 and c = 6.
    b) Calculate the value of b when a = 66 and c = 1.2.

6 **m is inversely proportional to the cube of n and m is equal to 20 when n is equal to 0.8.**
    a) Calculate the value of m when n is equal to 1.6.
    b) Calculate the value of n when m is equal to 20 000.

Exponential Growth and Decay

1 **A bacteria culture began with 4 000 bacteria. Each hour the number of bacteria increased by 10%.**

a) Complete the table below.

Time, t (hours)	0	1	2	3	4	5
Number of Bacteria, N	4000					

b) Draw the graph of Number of Bacteria against Time for the first 5 hours.

c) Use your graph to estimate the number of bacteria after $2\frac{1}{2}$ hours.

....

d) What formula shows the relationship between number of bacteria and time?

....

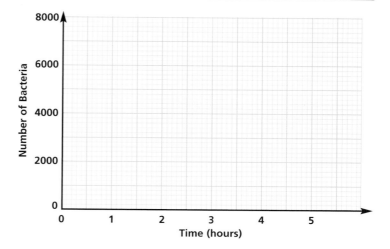

2 **The formula V = 8000 x 0.7^t gives the value of a car after t years.**

a) What is the value of the car when new?

....

b) What is the value of the car after 2 years?

....

c) Complete the table for the value of the car between 0 and 10 years.

Time	0	1	2	3	4	5	6	7	8	9	10
Value	8000										

d) Draw the graph of value (V) against time (t).

e) Estimate how long it takes for this car to halve in value ....

---

3 **Gnomes R Cool make 25 000 garden gnomes each year. The company wants to increase production by an extra 5% year on year.**
a) What is the relationship between the number of gnomes produced, N, and time, t, in years?
b) Draw a graph of number of gnomes produced against time for up to 5 years.
c) After how many complete years will Gnomes R Cool make 35 000 garden gnomes in a year?

4 **A rival company currently make 40 000 garden gnomes each year. Due to competition from Gnomes R Cool they plan to decrease production by 10% year on year. After how many complete years will Gnomes R Cool overtake this company in the yearly production of gnomes?**

The Basics of Algebra

1 Simplify...

a) $a + 2a$

b) $5x + 6x$

c) $11ab - 6ba$

d) $9p - 2p^2 + 4p$

e) $2a^2 + 3a^2 - 5a^2$

f) $10w^2 - w^2 + 2w^2$

g) $2a + 3b + 4a + 5b$

h) $7c - 8d - 9c + 10d$

i) $3a \times 2b$

j) $12pq \times 2r$

k) $4ab + 8cd - 7ab + cd + ab$

l) $-4x^2 + 6x + 7 + 3x^2 - 11x + 2$

m) $14 - 8p^2 + 11p + 2p^2 - 4p + 3$

n) $6pq^2 + 7p^2q - 5pq + 3p^2q - 7pq^2 + 4pq$

o) $4ab + 5bc + 6cd$

2 Simplify...

a) $a^2 \times a^3$

b) $4b^3 \times 3b$

c) $6p^4 \times 4p^6$

d) $r^6 \div r^2$

e) $12c^4 \div 3c^3$

f) $18a^2b \div 9a$

g) $15a^3b^2 \div 3ab$

h) $(2a^2 b)^3$

i) $y^5 \div y^2$

3 Simplify...

a) $\dfrac{8ab^2}{4b}$

b) $\dfrac{16a^3b^2}{ab^2}$

c) $\dfrac{(4ab)^2}{2ab^2}$

d) $\dfrac{12bc^2 \times 3ab^2}{4abc}$

---

4 Simplify...

a) $12x + 6x$ **b)** $12x - 6x$ **c)** $12x \times 6x$ **d)** $12x \div 6x$ **e)** $4p^2 - 11p^2$

f) $19ab - 13bc + 2ab + 16bc$ **g)** $13ab + 4a^2b - 2ab^2 + 3a^2b - 4ab + 10ab^2$

5 Simplify...

a) $a^4 \times a^3 \times a^2$ **b)** $2x^2 \times 3x \times 5x^5$ **c)** $16x^4 \div 16x^2$ **d)** $20a^3b^2c \div 10a^2b$ **e)** $(4a^2)^3$ **f)** $(3a^2b)^4$

1 If p = 2, q = 5 and r = -4, find the value of ...

   a) $2p + 3q$ ....

   b) $2(p + q)$ ....

   c) $2pq$ ....

   d) p^2q ....

   e) $pq - q^2$ ....

   f) pqr ....

   g) $p^3 + r^2$ ....

   h) $\dfrac{4p}{r}$ ....

   i) $p^2q^2 + \dfrac{r}{p}$ ....

   j) $\dfrac{p}{q} + \dfrac{r}{q}$ ....

2 If $x = \frac{1}{2}$, $y = \frac{1}{3}$ and z = -2, find the value of ...

   a) $x + y$ ....

   b) xz ....

   c) xz^2 ....

   d) $\dfrac{1}{x} + z$ ....

3 Find the value of ...

   a) $3x - 7$ when $x = -3$ ....

   b) $4(x^2 - 1)$ when $x = -3$ ....

   c) $4(x - 1)^2$ when $x = 5$ ....

   d) $(x + 2)(x - 3)$ when $x = 6$ ....

   e) $(x^2 - 5)(x + 8)$ when $x = -5$ ....

---

4 If e = 3, f = 8, g = -4 and h = $\frac{1}{4}$, find the value of ...
   a) ef **b)** fg **c)** gh **d)** $e + f + g$ **e)** $f + g + h$ **f)** $e^2 - f$ **g)** g^2h **h)** $f \div g$ **i)** $e^3 + g$ **j)** $2f \div g^2$ **k)** $\frac{1}{e} + h$ **l)** $e^2 + f + g^2$

5 Find the value of ...
   a) $5x^2 - 3$ when $x = -4$ **b)** $5(x - 3)$ when $x = -4$ **c)** $5x^2 - 3$ when $x = -2$ **d)** $(x + 3)(2x - 1)$ when $x = 2$
   e) $(x^2 + 3)(x - 5)$ when $x = -1$

6 If $m = 3 \times 10^4$ and $n = 5 \times 10^3$, find the value of...

   a) mn **b)** m+n **c)** $\dfrac{mn}{m+n}$

   Give your answers in standard form to 2 significant figures.

Brackets and Factorisation

1 **Expand and simplify ...**

a) $4(2x + 1)$

b) $3(3r - 7)$

c) $2m(3m + 2)$

d) $2p(4 - p)$

e) $6r(r^2 - 3)$

f) $10x(4x^2 - 3x)$

g) $5(2y + 4) + 3$

h) $5x(2 - 3x) + 7x$

i) $11x(5 - 3x^2) - 9x$

j) $5(3x + 2) + 4(x - 3)$

k) $5(6x + 1) + 3(4x - 2)$

l) $5x(2x - 3) - 4(3x - 1)$

m) $(x + 2)(x + 5)$

n) $(2x + 3)(x + 4)$

o) $(3x - 2)(2x + 1)$

p) $(4x - 1)(x - 5)$

q) $(x + 3)(x - 3)$

r) $(4x - 1)^2$

2 **Factorise the following expressions:**

a) $5x + 10$

b) $4x - 8$

c) $6x + 10y$

d) $6x + 3x^2$

e) $10x^2 - 5x$

f) $6x^2y - 10xy$

g) $4p^2q^3r + 6pqr$

h) $x(3y + 2) + z(3y + 2)$

i) $x(4y + 3) + (4y + 3)^2$

3 **Expand and simplify ...**
   a) $6(4x - y)$ **b)** $3x(2x + 5)$ **c)** $4x^2(2y - x)$ **d)** $6x(3 - x^2)$ **e)** $4(2x + 3) + 5(x - 7)$ **f)** $6x(2x - 3) + 4(x + 5)$
   g) $10x^2(4x + 3) - 6x(2x - 1)$ **h)** $(4x + 2)(3x + 2)$ **i)** $(5x + 6)(5x - 6)$ **j)** $(4x^2 + 3x)(2x + 2)$ **k)** $(2x^3 - 3)(4 - 3x^2)$

4 **Factorise the following expressions:**
   a) $9x - 15$ **b)** $9x + 9$ **c)** $20x^2 - x$ **d)** $4x - 20x^3$ **e)** $20x^2y^2 + 36xy$ **f)** $4(3x - 5) + y(3x - 5)$

5 **a)** Expand and simplify $(a + b)^2$ **b)** Without using a calculator work out the value of $8.8^2 + 2 \times 8.8 \times 1.2 + 1.2^2$

Solving Equations 1 & 2

1 Solve the following equations:

a) $5x = 35$

b) $3x + 4 = 16$

c) $5x + 8 = 23$

d) $2(x + 2) = 12$

e) $5(x - 3) = 10$

f) $4(5 + 3x) = 14$

g) $\dfrac{x}{3} = 6$

h) $\dfrac{x}{2} + \dfrac{x}{6} = 10$

i) $\dfrac{x + 2}{5} = 3$

j) $5x = 2x + 9$

k) $7x = 15 - 3x$

l) $2x = x - 8$

m) $11x + 3 = 3x + 7$

n) $5 + 7x = 23 + 3x$

o) $10x - 6 = 3x + 15$

p) $8(3x - 2) = 20$

q) $5(x + 7) = 3(9 + x)$

r) $\dfrac{x + 1}{2} + \dfrac{x - 3}{4} = 2$

s) $\dfrac{5x + 4}{3} + \dfrac{8 - x}{2} = 10$

t) $\dfrac{9x + 10}{4} - \dfrac{4x - 4}{10} = 14$

u) $\dfrac{x}{x + 1} - \dfrac{2}{x - 1} = 1$

Solving Equations 1 & 2

2 **Maggie is x years old.**   **Nigel is twice Maggie's age.**   **Helen is 4 years older than Nigel.**

  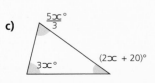

a) Write down an expression in terms of x for their combined age.

....

....

....

b) Their total combined age is 64 years. Form an equation and solve it to find Helen's age.

....

....

....

3 ABC is a triangle:

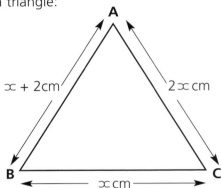

a) Write down an expression in terms of x for the perimeter of the triangle.

....

....

b) The perimeter of triangle ABC is 50cm. Form an equation and solve it to find x.

....

....

....

4 ABCD is a rectangle:

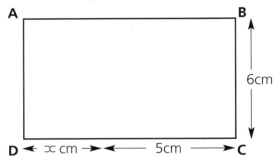

a) Write down an expression in terms of x for the area of the rectangle.

....

....

b) The area of rectangle ABCD is 72cm². Form an equation and solve it to find x.

....

....

....

5 **Solve the following equations to find the value of x:**

a) $2x + 5 = 17$ **b)** $15 + 3x = 3$ **c)** $4x = x + 18$ **d)** $10x = 7x - 15$ **e)** $4x - 3 = 6x + 12$ **f)** $9x + 7 = 4x - 13$

g) $14 + 5x = 7x + 2$ **h)** $23 - 8x = x - 4$ **i)** $40x - 36 = 7x + 30$ **j)** $4(x + 5) = 36$ **k)** $7(2x - 3) = 14$ **l)** $6 = 4(3x - 9)$

m) $16 = 4(11 - 5x)$ **n)** $5(x + 1) = 2(x + 7)$ **o)** $11(3x + 2) = (6x - 5)$ **p)** $9(2x + 4) - 4(5x + 8) = 0$

q) $\dfrac{x - 10}{10} + \dfrac{2x + 1}{5} = 0.7$ **r)** $\dfrac{4x + 6}{2} - \dfrac{10x}{15} = 5$

6 **For each of the following form an equation and solve it to find x.**

a)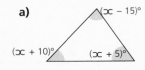

b)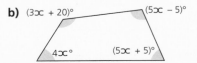

c)

Formulae 1 & 2

1 **Rearrange the following formulae to make x the subject:**

a) $x + 4y = 3$

b) $6x + 7y = 50$

c) $7x - 5 = 3y$

d) $\dfrac{x}{y} + 5 = z$

e) $\dfrac{x + 3y}{4} = 5$

f) $\dfrac{4x - 3}{y} = 8$

g) $5x + 3y = 3(6 - x)$

h) $4x^2 = 3y$

i) $\dfrac{x^2}{3} = 6y$

j) $5x^2 + 3 = 7y$

2 **The volume of a cone is given by the formula: volume = $\frac{1}{3}\pi r^2 h$.**

Calculate the volume of a cone in cm³ if r = 4cm, h = 10cm and π = 3.

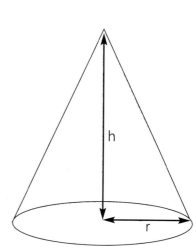

Formulae 1 & 2 (cont)

3 The distance travelled (s) by an object depends on its initial speed (u), its final speed (v) and the time of travel (t). It is given by the formula:

$$s = \left(\frac{u + v}{2}\right) t$$

Calculate the distance travelled in metres if initial speed = 4m/s, final speed = 12m/s and time = 5.5s.

....

....

4 Make r the subject of the formula.

$$r - 6 = 2\pi \, (p - 4r)$$

....

....

....

....

5 The circumference of a circle is given by the formula $C = 2\pi r$, where r is the radius.

The area of a circle is given by the formula $A = \pi r^2$.

a) Generate a formula for the area of a circle in terms of its circumference, C.

....

....

....

b) Use your formula to work out the area of a circle in cm^2, which has a circumference of 40cm and $\pi = 3.14$. Give your answer to two significant figures.

....

....

---

6 Rearrange the following formulae to make p the subject:
a) $4p - 3 = 4q$ **b)** $4 - 6p = q$ **c)** $3(2p + 5) = 4p + 11q$ **d)** $3p^2 + 4 = 8q$ **e)** $\dfrac{3p^2 - 6}{4} = 2q$

7 The area of a parallelogram is given by the formula: Area = length x height.
Calculate the area, in m^2, of a parallelogram that has length = 90cm and height = 1.2m.

8 The area, A, of a circle is given by the formula: $A = \pi r^2$, where r is the radius.
Calculate the radius if area = $100cm^2$ and $\pi = 3.14$. Give your answer to two significant figures.

9 A garden centre buys shrubs at wholesale prices. They calculate the sale price (s), at which they are sold to customers, by increasing the wholesale price (w) by 50% and adding £2.50 per shrub.
a) Generate a formula for calculating the sale price of a shrub.
b) If the wholesale price of a shrub is £4.00, use your formula to calculate its sale price.

Quadratic Expressions 1

1 **Factorise the following quadratic expressions:**

a) $x^2 + 6x + 8$

b) $x^2 + 7x + 10$

c) $x^2 + 6x + 9$

d) $x^2 - 9x + 20$

e) $x^2 + 9x - 10$

f) $x^2 + 8x - 20$

g) $x^2 - x - 12$

h) $x^2 - 10x - 24$

i) $x^2 - 9$

j) $x^2 - 64$

k) $x^2 - 100$

l) $x^2 - 144$

---

2 **Factorise the following quadratic expressions:**
a) $x^2 + 5x + 6$ **b)** $x^2 - 5x + 6$ **c)** $x^2 + 5x - 6$ **d)** $x^2 - 5x - 6$
e) $x^2 + x - 30$ **f)** $x^2 + 31x + 30$ **g)** $x^2 - 81$ **h)** $x^2 - 169$

Quadratic Expressions 2

1 **Factorise the following quadratic expressions:**

a) $2x^2 + 5x - 3$

b) $4x^2 + 3x - 1$

c) $2x^2 + 7x + 3$

d) $6x^2 + x - 2$

e) $6y^2 - 11y - 10$

f) $12n^2 - 11n + 2$

g) $20x^2 + 27x - 14$

h) $25x^2 - 30x + 9$

i) $49x^2 + 14x + 1$

2 **Factorise the following quadratic expressions completely. You may need to rearrange them first.**

a) $5a^2 + 15a - 20$

b) $12n^2 + 39n + 9$

c) $8x^2 + 2 - 8x$

d) $2x^2 + 2 + 4x$

e) $n + 3n^2 - 4$

f) $2x^2 - 3 - x$

3 **Rearrange the expression $3 - 5x - 2x^2$ then factorise.**

4 **Rearrange the following expressions where necessary then factorise completely:**
a) $42 - 34n + 4n^2$ **b)** $25y^2 + 4 - 20y$ **c)** $11x - 6x^2 - 3$

5 **a)** Factorise $7n^2 + 52n + 21$
b) Use your result from part a) to write 75 221 as a product of two prime numbers. Explain your reasoning.
c) The number 32 207 is the product of two prime numbers. What expression could you factorise to find these prime numbers?

Quadratic Equations 1 & 2

1 **Factorise these quadratic equations and then solve them.**

a) $a^2 + a - 6 = 0$

....

....

....

b) $a^2 + 4a - 5 = 0$

....

....

....

c) $a^2 - 2a - 8 = 0$

....

....

....

d) $2a^2 - 5a - 3 = 0$

....

....

....

e) $3a^2 + 14a + 8 = 0$

....

....

....

f) $8a^2 + 6a - 9 = 0$

....

....

....

2 **Solve these equations, rearranging them first.**

a) $x^2 + 5x = 6$

....

....

....

....

b) $x^2 + 28 = 11y$

....

....

....

....

c) $x^2 - 3x + 3 = 1$

....

....

....

....

3 **A rectangle has dimensions as shown in the diagram opposite. The area of the rectangle is 80cm².**

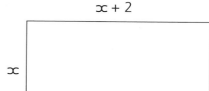

$x + 2$

a) Write an equation for the area.

....

b) Solve this equation.

....

....

c) Find the perimeter of the rectangle. ....

4 **The squares of two consecutive whole numbers add up to 61. Let _n_ be the first number.**

a) Write an expression for the second number. ....

b) Write an equation for the sum of the squares of the two consecutive numbers.

....

c) Solve the equation to find the two whole numbers.

....

....

....

Quadratic Equations 1 & 2 (cont)

5 Find the solutions of these equations (to 2 d.p.) by completing the square.

a) $x^2 + 10x - 4 = 0$

b) $x^2 - 10x + 1 = 0$

c) $x^2 - 4x - 3 = 0$

6 Annika's vegetable plot has dimensions as shown in the diagram. She decides to increase the size of the plot by adding x metres to the length and width.

a) Write down an expression for the area of the entire enlarged plot, multiplying out any brackets.

b) Write an expression for the area of the extension only.

c) Find x if Annika increases the area by 104m².

7 Find the values of p and q such that $x^2 - 20x + 27 = (x - p)^2 + q$

8 Solve these equations by either factorising or completing the square.
a) $x^2 - 7x + 3 = 0$ **b)** $4a^2 - 19a + 12 = 0$ **c)** $x^2 - x - 6 = 14$
d) $x^2 + 12x - 5 = 0$ **e)** $35 - 2a = a^2$ **f)** $4y^2 - 8y + 3 = 0$

9 The difference between the square of a number and the number itself is 72. Write down and solve an equation to find the two possible values of the number.

10 The sum of the first 'n' numbers in the sequence '1, 2, 3, 4 ...' is given by the formula $\frac{n}{2}(n + 1)$. How many numbers must be taken to give a sum of 55?

Quadratic Equations 3

1 Find the solutions to these quadratic equations (to 2 d.p.). You may need to rearrange them first.

a) $2x^2 + 3x - 1 = 0$

b) $2 - 3x - x^2 = 0$

c) $5x^2 + 4x = 2$

....

....

....

....

....

....

....

....

....

....

....

....

2 In the triangle opposite AC is 2m shorter than AB.

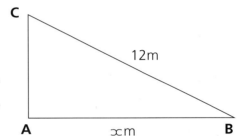

a) Using Pythagoras' theorem write down an equation for x.

....

....

b) Show how this can be simplified to $x^2 - 2x - 70 = 0$.

....

....

....

c) Solve this equation using the quadratic formula.

....

....

....

....

3 Solve the following equations to 1 d.p. using the quadratic formula.
a) $x(x + 2) = 5$ **b)** $x^2 = 4x - 3$ **c)** $(x + 1)(x - 2) = 3$
d) $x^2 + 10x - 4 = 0$ **e)** $3x^2 - 3x = 2$ **f)** $4 - 5x - x^2 = 0$

4 A square picture of side 20cm is put in a frame w cm wide.
a) Write an expression for the area of the frame in terms of w.
b) If the picture has an area of half the area of the frame and picture together, write an equation for w.
c) Show that this equation can be simplified to $w^2 + 20w - 100 = 0$
d) Solve the equation to find the width of the frame (w) to 1 d.p.

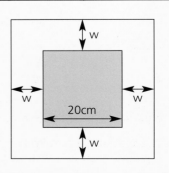

Trial and Improvement

1 The equation $x^3 - x = 15$ has a solution which lies between 2 and 3. Using trial and improvement complete the table to solve the equation and find x. Give your answer correct to 1 decimal place.

x	$x^3 - x$	Comment
2	$2^3 - 2 = 8 - 2 = 6$	Less than 15
3	$3^3 - 3 = 27 - 3 = 24$	More than 15

Answer: ....

2 The equation $x^3 + 2x = 40$ has a solution which lies between 3 and 4. By trial and improvement calculate a solution to 2 decimal places.

x	$x^3 + 2x$	Comment

Answer: ....

3 A rectangular box has the following dimensions:

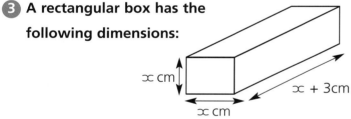

x cm

x cm

$x + 3$cm

a) Show that the volume of the box is given by the expression $x^3 + 3x^2$.

....

....

b) The volume of the box is 40cm³. Using trial and improvement, find x which has a value that lies between 2 and 3. Give your answer to 1 decimal place.

x	$x^3 + 3x^2$	Comment

Answer: ....

4 **a)** The equation $x^3 + 10x = 24$ has one solution which lies between 1 and 2.
Using trial and improvement, find the solution to 1 decimal place.
b) The equation $x^3 - 6x = 65$ has one solution which lies between 4 and 5.
Using trial and improvement, find the solution to 2 decimal places.

5 Use trial and improvement to find a solution to the equation...

$$2x + \frac{2}{x} = 7 \text{ (to 1 d.p.)}$$

Number Patterns & Sequences 1 & 2

1 **a)** The first four numbers of a sequence are:

1, 3, 7, 15...

The rule to continue this sequence of numbers is:

**Multiply the previous
number by 2 and
then add 1**

i) What are the next two numbers in the sequence?

....

ii) The following sequence obeys the same rule:

-2, -3, -5, -9...

What are the next two numbers in this sequence?

....

b) The first four numbers of a sequence are:

3, 4, 6, 10...

The rule to continue this sequence of numbers is:

**Subtract 1 from the
previous number and
then multiply by 2**

i) What are the next two numbers in the sequence?

....

ii) The following sequence obeys the same rule:

1, 0, -2, -6...

What are the next two numbers in this sequence?

....

2 **a)** The first four square numbers are 1, 4, 9 and 16. What are the next four numbers in the sequence?

....

b) The first four triangular numbers are 1, 3, 6 and 10. What are the next four numbers in the sequence?

....

3 **The nth term of a sequence is 5n + 8.**

a) What is the value of the 3rd term?

....

b) What is the value of the 10th term?

....

4 **The nth term of a sequence is 2n – 11.**

a) What is the value of the 4th term?

....

b) What is the value of the 16th term?

....

5 **The nth term of a sequence is 2n – 9.**

a) Which term has a value of 19?

....

....

b) Which term has a value of -5?

....

....

6 **The nth term of a sequence is 7n + 6.**

a) Which term has a value of 69?

....

....

b) Which term has a value of 90?

....

....

Number Patterns & Sequences 1 & 2

7 The first four terms of a sequence are:

3, 5, 7, 9, ...

Write down a formula for the nth term of this sequence and add a further 5 terms to the sequence in the space above.

....

....

....

....

8 The first four terms of a sequence are:

6, 4, 2, 0, ...

Write down a formula for the nth term of this sequence and add a further 5 terms to the sequence in the space above.

....

....

....

....

9 Here is a sequence of diagrams made up of squares:

Diagram 1   **Diagram 2**   **Diagram 3**   **Diagram 4**

a) Write down a formula for the number of squares (s) in terms of diagram number (n).

....

....

....

b) How many squares would there be in Diagram 8?

....

c) Which number diagram would have 49 squares?

....

10 Here is a sequence of diagrams made up of circles:

Diagram 1   **Diagram 2**   **Diagram 3**   **Diagram 4**

a) Write down a formula for the number of circles (c) in terms of diagram number (n).

....

....

....

b) How many circles would there be in Diagram 15?

....

c) Which number diagram would have 81 circles?

....

11 Draw the next two diagrams of the following sequences:

a)   **b)**

12 The nth term of a sequence is $\frac{(4n-7)}{3}$ **a)** What is the value of the 10th term? **b)** Which term has a value of 27?

13 The first four terms of a sequence are: **15, 11, 7, 3**

a) Write down a formula for the nth term of this sequence. **b)** What is the value of ... **i)** the 10th term? **ii)** the 100th term?

Graphs of Linear Functions 1

1 On the axes provided, draw and label the graphs of the following linear functions for values of x between -2 and 2:

a) $y = 2x$

x	-2	0	2
y	-4	0	4

d) $y = -2x$

x			
y			

b) $y = 2x - 1$

x	-2	0	2
y	-5		

e) $y = -x - 3$

x			
y			

c) $y = x + 2$

x			
y			

2 a) Make y the subject of the following function:

$2y - x = 8$

....

....

b) On the axes provided, draw and label the graph of the rearranged function from part a).

x			
y			

c) A point, which lies on the line of the graph that you have just drawn, has the coordinates (5,p). Calculate the value of p.

....

....

d) Another point that lies on the line of the drawn graph has the coordinates (q, 0). Calculate the value of q.

....

....

---

3 **a)** Make y the subject of the following function: $y - 3x = -4$
b) Draw the graph of the rearranged function for values of x between -3 and 3.
c) Use the graph to calculate the value of y if $x = 1.5$
d) Use the graph to calculate the value of x if $y = 3.2$

4 **a)** Draw graphs of $y = 3x$ and $y = x + 5$ for values of x between 0 and 3 on the same set of axes.
b) What is the x coordinate of the point where the two lines cross?

Graphs of Linear Functions 2

1 **Find the gradient and intercept of the following linear functions:**

a) $y = 2x + 1$

....

....

....

b) $y = 3x - 1$

....

....

....

c) $x + y = 3$

....

....

....

d) $4y = 7 - 8x$

....

....

....

e) $2y - 2x = 9$

....

....

....

f) $2x = y - 2$

....

....

....

2 **On the axes below are the graphs of four lines whose equations can be found in question 1. What is the equation of each line?**

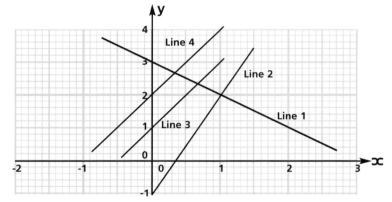

Line 1: ....

Line 2: ....

Line 3: ....

Line 4: ....

3 **What is the equation of the line which crosses the y-axis at ...**

a) $(0,1)$ and is parallel to $y = 2x$? ....

b) $(0,1)$ and is parallel to $y = -2x$? ....

c) $(0,-2)$ and is parallel to $y = 2x$? ....

d) $(0,-2)$ and is parallel to $y = x + 2$? ....

e) $(0,3)$ and is perpendicular to $y = -x - 3$? ....

f) $(0,-3.5)$ and is perpendicular to $y = -x$? ....

---

4 **Find the gradient and intercept of the following linear functions:**
a) $y = -3x - 3$ **b)** $4y = 3x + 8$ **c)** $2y - x = 3$ **d)** $x - 2y = 3$ **e)** $2y - 3 = x$ **f)** $\frac{y - 2x}{3} = 5$ **g)** $\frac{y + 4x}{5} = 1$

5 **What is the equation of the line which crosses the y-axis at ...**
a) $(0, 4)$ and is parallel to $y = x - 4$ **b)** $(0, 0)$ and is perpendicular to $y = x - 4$

6 **Which of the following linear functions would produce parallel lines if drawn on the same axes:**
i) $y = 2x + 3$ **ii)** $y + 2x = 3$ **iii)** $2y - 4x = 7$ **iv)** $y - 6 = 2x$

7 **Which of the following linear functions would produce perpendicular lines if drawn on the same axes:**
i) $y - 2x = 4$ **ii)** $3x + y = 7$ **iii)** $3y - x = 4$ **iv)** $3y + 3x = 5$

Graphs of Linear Functions 3

1 Find the gradient, intercept and equation of the following lines:

a)

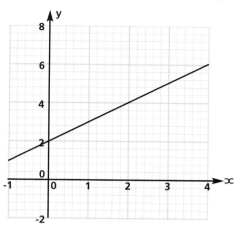

....
....
....
....
....
....

b)

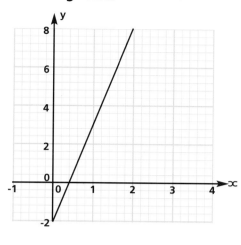

....
....
....
....
....
....

c)

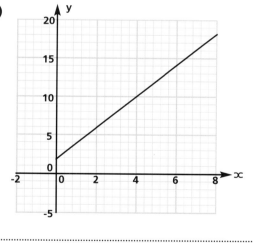

....
....
....
....
....
....

d)

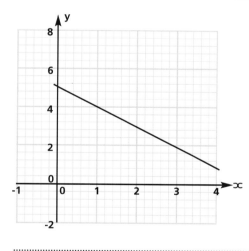

....
....
....
....
....
....

2 Plot the following points: A (0,1), B (4,5), C (1,4) and D (4,1).
  a) Calculate the gradient of **i)** line AB, **ii)** line CD, **b)** What is the equation of **i)** line AB, **ii)** line CD?

3 A line has intercept c = +2. A point with coordinates (4,4) lies on the line. What is the equation of the line?

4 A line has intercept c = +5. A point with coordinates (4,1) lies on the line. What is the equation of the line?

Three Special Graphs

1 On the axes below are the graphs of 6 lines. What is the equation of each line?

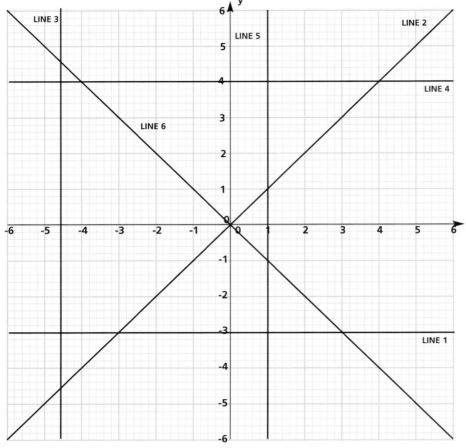

Line 1 ....

Line 2 ....

Line 3 ....

Line 4 ....

Line 5 ....

Line 6 ....

2 **a)** Two points which lie on the line of a drawn graph have coordinates (-3,0) and (4,0).

What is the equation of the line? ....

b) Two points which lie on the line of a drawn graph have coordinates (-1,5) and (-1,3).

What is the equation of the line? ....

c) Two points which lie on the line of a drawn graph have coordinates (-4,4) and (4,-4).

What is the equation of the line? ....

3 **What is the equation of the line that passes through the point with coordinates (3,3) and has a gradient of 1?** ....

4 **a)** What are the coordinates of the point of intersection of the two lines $y = x$ and $y = -3$?

....

b) What are the coordinates of the point of intersection of the two lines $y = 6$ and $x = -2$?

....

5 **What is the equation of the line that is parallel to the x-axis and passes through the point with coordinates (2.5, 3.6)?**

6 **What is the equation of the line that is perpendicular to the x-axis and passes through the point with coordinates (-2.8, 1.2)?**

Linear Inequalities 1 & 2

1 Solve the following inequalities and draw a number line for each one.

a) $x + 2 > 11$

b) $8 > x - 9$

c) $2x + 5 \leqslant 15$

d) $13 \geqslant 5 + 4x$

e) $7x - 2 \leqslant 2x + 13$

f) $-6 \leqslant 3x < 9$

2 Solve the following inequalities:

a) $12 + 3x < 6$

b) $14 > 5 - 3x$

c) $5(4x + 7) \geqslant 15$

d) $3(2x + 5) \geqslant 24$

e) $6(4 - x) \leqslant 9$

f) $8 \geqslant 3 - 2x$

3 Draw, label and shade the region represented by each inequality on the grids provided.

a) $x \geqslant 1$

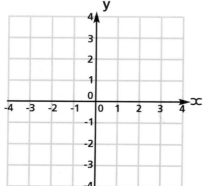

b) $y < -2$

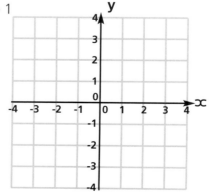

c) $y > -x + 2$

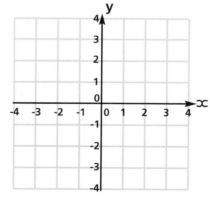

d) $y \leqslant 2x - 1$

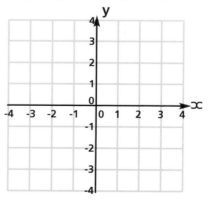

Linear Inequalities 1 & 2 (cont)

4 a) On the grid, draw and shade the region that satisfies these three inequalities:

$x \leqslant 3$, $y \leqslant 4$ and $x + y \geqslant 4$

Label the region A.

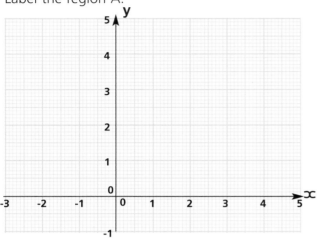

b) B is a point within region A, which has coordinates that are both integers.
What are the coordinates of B?

....

5 a) On the grid, draw and shade the region that satisfies these three inequalities:

$x < 4$, $y \geqslant 1$ and $x < y$

Label the region A.

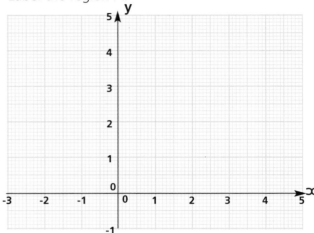

b) B is a point within region A, which has coordinates that are both integers.
What are the coordinates of B?

....

6 On the grid, draw and shade the region that satisfies these four inequalities:

$x > -2$, $y \geqslant 0$, $y \geqslant 0.5x$, $x + y < 3$

Label the region A.

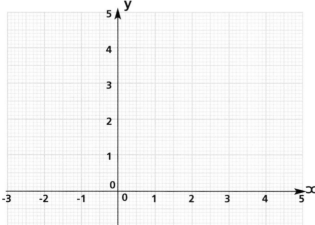

7 On the grid, the region labelled A satisfies four inequalities, what are they?

....

....

8 Solve the following inequalities and for each one draw a number line. **a)** $4x \geqslant 20$ **b)** $x + 3 > 5$ **c)** $4x - 3 \leqslant 19$
d) $8x + 5 < 2x - 7$ **e)** $5(2x - 3) < 4x + 9$ **f)** $7(3x - 2) \geqslant 20x - 16$ **g)** $6(3x - 2) < 4(4x - 10)$

9 On a suitable grid, draw and shade the region that satisfies these three inequalities:
$x \geqslant 2$, $y \leqslant 5$ and $y \geqslant x$. **Label the region A.**

10 On a suitable grid, draw and shade the region that satisfies these four inequalities:
$x > -1$, $y \geqslant x - 2$, $y > -1$ and $y \leqslant -x + 5$. **Label the region A.**

Simultaneous Equations 1

1 Solve the following simultaneous equations:

a) $2x + y = 8$

$x + y = 5$

b) $2x + 5y = 24$

$3x - 5y = 11$

c) $x - 6y = 17$

$3x + 2y = 11$

d) $4x + 3y = 27$

$x + y = 7$

e) $5x - 2y = 14$

$2x + 3y = 17$

f) $3x + 4y = 13$

$2x - 3y = 3$

2 At break time a student buys two doughnuts and a coffee which cost her 84p altogether. At lunchtime, the same student buys three doughnuts and two coffees which cost 138p altogether. Form two equations with the information given and work out the individual price of a doughnut (d) and a coffee (c).

3 Solve the following simultaneous equations:

a) $5x + y = 14$, $3x + y = 10$ **b)** $4x - y = 6$, $x + y = 9$ **c)** $3x + 2y = 8$, $x + y = 2$ **d)** $4x + 6y = 12$, $x + y = 1$

e) $4x + 2y = 13$, $10x - 4y = 1$ **f)** $x - 10y = 2$, $4x + 2y = -13$ **g)** $4x - 3y = -6$, $y - 3x = 7$ **h)** $10x + 2y = 0$, $x - y = 9$

Simultaneous Equations 2

1 a) On the axes below, draw and label the graph of the following equations:

y = x + 8 and y = 2x + 5

x	0	2	4
y=x+8	8	10	12

x	0	2	4
y=2x+5	5	9	13

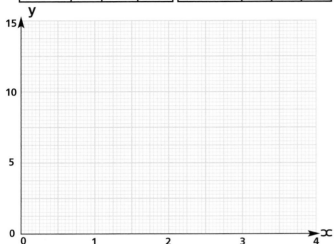

b) Use your graph to solve the simultaneous equations: y = x + 8 and y = 2x + 5

....

2 a) On the axes below, draw and label the graph of the following equations:

y = 3x + 10 and y = -x + 22

x	0	2	4
y=3x+10			

x	0	2	4
y=-x+22			

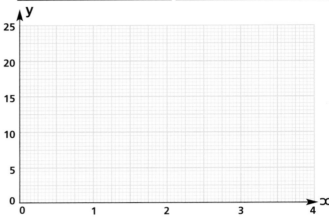

b) Use your graph to solve the simultaneous equations: y = 3x + 10 and y = -x + 22

....

3 a) On the axes provided draw the graphs of the following lines:

i) y = -x + 4

ii) y = x + 2

iii) y = -0.25x + 1

b) Use your graph to solve the following simultaneous equations:

i) y = x + 2 and y = -0.25x + 1 ....

ii) y = x + 2 and y = -x + 4 ....

iii) y = -x + 4 and y = -0.25x + 1 ....

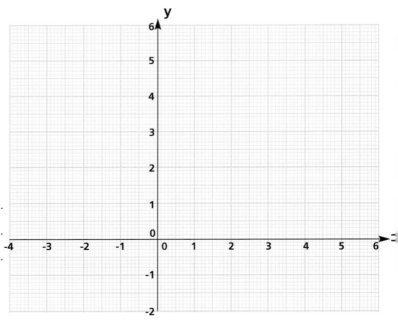

4 a) Draw the graph of 2x + y = 13 and 3x = y − 3 for values of x between 0 and 4.
   b) Use your graph to solve the simultaneous equations 2x + y = 13 and 3x = y − 3.

5 a) Draw the graph of x + y = 6, 3x − y = 2 and x − y = 4 for values of x between -2 and 6.
   b) Use your graph to solve the following simultaneous equations:
   i) x + y = 6, 3x − y = 2 **ii)** x + y = 6, x − y = 4 **iii)** 3x − y = 2, x − y = 4.

Simultaneous Equations 3 & 4

1 **Solve these simultaneous equations (to 1 d.p.).**

a) $y = 3 - 14x$ and $y = 5x^2$

b) $y = 10x^2$ and $y = x + 24$

2 **Solve these simultaneous equations by substitution. If need be give your answers to 2 d.p.**

a) $x^2 + y^2 = 1$ and $x + y = 1$

b) $x^2 + y^2 = 9$ and $x + y = 2$

Simultaneous Equations 3 & 4

3 **a)** Using the axes opposite solve graphically the simultaneous equations $y - x = 1$ and $y = x^2$

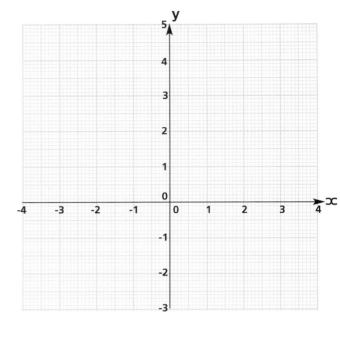

....

....

....

b) Check your answers to part a) by substituting your values for x and y into the equations.

....

....

....

4 **Using the axes opposite solve graphically these pairs of simultaneous equations:**

a) $x^2 + y^2 = 9$
   $y - x = 2$

b) $x^2 + y^2 = 9$
   $x + y = 2$

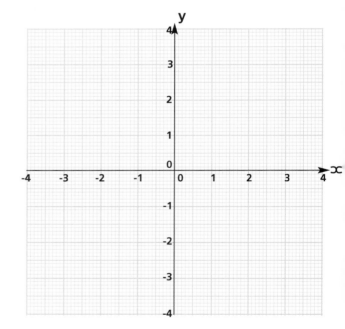

....

....

....

5 **a)** Solve these simultaneous equations graphically. If need be, give your answer to 1 d.p.
b) Check your answers by substituting the values for x and y into the equations.

i) $y = 2x^2$ **ii)** $y = \frac{1}{2}x^2$ **iii)** $y = x^2$
   $y - x = 2$ $x + y = 1$ $x + y = 1$

6 **Solve graphically the following simultaneous equations:**
a) $x^2 + y^2 = 4$ **b)** $x^2 + y^2 = 9$ **c)** $x^2 + y^2 = 1$
   $y = 2x$ $y = -x + 2$ $y = \frac{1}{2}x^2$

7 **a)** Show that the x coordinates of A and B are given by the solutions to the equation $2x^2 + 4x - 5 = 0$
b) Solve the equation $2x^2 + 4x - 5 = 0$

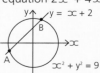

Graphs of Quadratic Funcs. 1 & 2

1 **Below is a table of values for** $y = x^2 - 2$.

x	-2	-1	0	1	2
y	2	-1	-2	-1	2

a) Draw the graph of $y = x^2 - 2$.

b) From your graph find the value(s) of...

i) y when $x = 1.5$

....

ii) x when $y = 1.5$

....

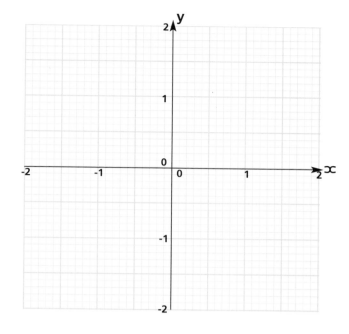

2 **Below is a half-completed table of values for**

$y = x^2 + x - 3$.

a) Complete the table.

x	-3	-2	-1	0	1	2
x^2		4		0		4
+x		-2		0		2
-3		-3		-3		-3
$y = x^2 + x - 3$		-1		-3		3

b) Draw the graph of $y = x^2 + x - 3$.

c) From your graph find the value(s) of...

i) y when $x = -2.5$

....

ii) x when $y = 1.6$

....

d) From your graph find the solution to the

equation $x^2 + x - 3 = 0$.

....

e) From your graph find the solution to the

equation $x^2 + x - 3 = 1$.

....

f) From your graph find the solution to the

equation $x^2 + x - 3 = -2$.

....

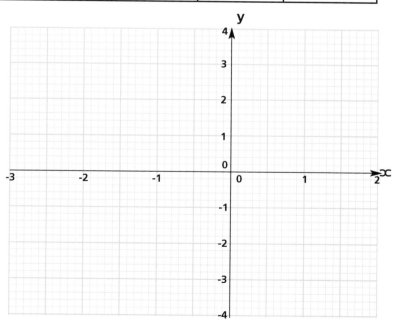

Graphs of Quadratic Funcs. 1 & 2

3 a) Complete the table for $y = x^2 - 3x - 4$.

x	-2	-1	0	1	2	3	4	5
y	6		-4			-4		

b) Draw the graph of $y = x^2 - 3x - 4$.

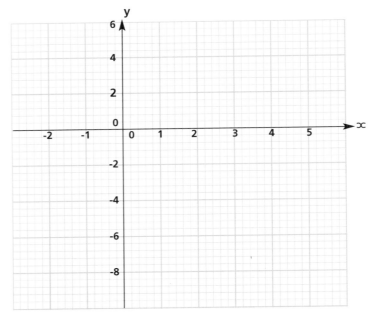

c) From the graph find the solutions to the equation ...

$x^2 - 3x - 4 = 0$

....

....

....

....

d) Find the solutions of $x^2 - 3x - 4 = 0$ by factorising to check your answers for c).

....

....

---

4 a) Draw a table of results for $y = x^2 + 4x - 6$ for values of x between -6 and 2.
b) Draw the graph of $y = x^2 + 4x - 6$.
c) From your graph find the solutions to the equations ...
i) $x^2 + 4x - 6 = 0$ **ii)** $x^2 + 4x - 9 = 0$ **iii)** $x^2 + 4x + 2 = 0$

5 a) Draw the graph of $y = x^2 - 12$ for values of x between -4 and 4.
b) From your graph find the solutions to the equations ...
i) $x^2 - 12 = 0$ **ii)** $x^2 = 15$ **iii)** $x^2 - 6 = 0$

6 **The diagram shows the graph of the form $y = x^2 + bx + c$.**
Find the values of b and c.

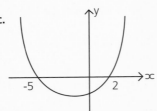

Graphs of Other Functions 1

1 Below is a half-completed table of values for $y = x^3 + 10$.

a) Complete the table.

x	-3	-2	-1	0	1	2
x^3		-8		0		8
+10		+10		+10		+10
$y = x^3 + 10$		2		10		18

b) On the axes opposite draw the graph of $y = x^3 + 10$.

c) Use your graph to find ...

i) the value of x, when $y = -10$

....

ii) the value of y, when $x = 1.5$

....

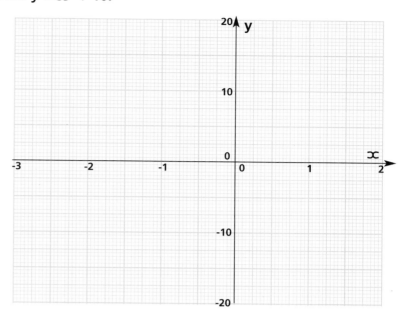

2 Below is a table of values for $y = \frac{1}{x}$ with $x \neq 0$.

x	-5	-4	-3	-2	-1	-0.5	-0.$\dot{3}$	-0.25	-0.2
$y=\frac{1}{x}$	-0.2	-0.25	-0.$\dot{3}$	-0.5	-1	-2	-3	-4	-5

x	0.2	0.25	0.$\dot{3}$	0.5	1	2	3	4	5
$y=\frac{1}{x}$	5	4	3	2	1	0.5	0.$\dot{3}$	0.25	0.2

a) On the axes opposite draw the graph of $y = \frac{1}{x}$ with $x \neq 0$.

b) Use your graph to find...

i) the value of x when $y = 2.5$ ....

ii) the value of y when $x = -1.5$............................

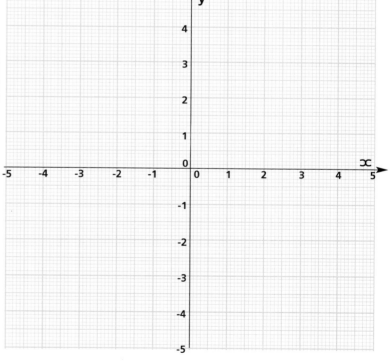

3 Below is a half-completed table of values for $y = x^3 - 2$.

x	-3	-2	-1	0	1	2	3
x^3		-8		0		8	
-2		-2		-2		-2	
$y = x^3 - 2$		-10		-2		6	

a) Complete the table.

b) Draw the graph of $y = x^3 - 2$.

c) Use your graph to find the value of x, when $y = 0$

d) Use your graph to find...

i) the value of x when $y = 20$

ii) the value of y when $x = 1.5$

Graphs of Other Functions 2

1 **a)** For values of x from -2 to 2 complete the tables below.

x	-2	-1	0	1	2
4^x					

x	-2	-1	0	1	2
$\left(\frac{1}{4}\right)^x$					

b) Draw graphs of $y = 4x$ and $y = \left(\frac{1}{4}\right)^x$ on the same axes opposite.

c) What do you notice about the two functions?

....

....

....

....

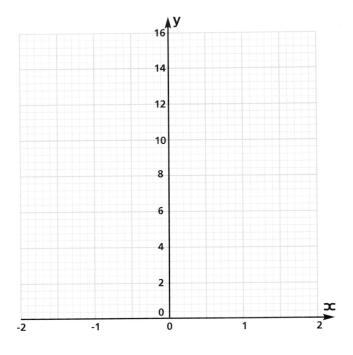

2 **a)** The table below shows values of x and y for the relationship $y = ab^x$.

x	0	1	2	3
y	10	20	40	80

b) Using the axes opposite draw the graph of the relationship $y = ab^x$.

c) Use the graph to find the values of **a** and **b** and the relationship.

....

....

....

....

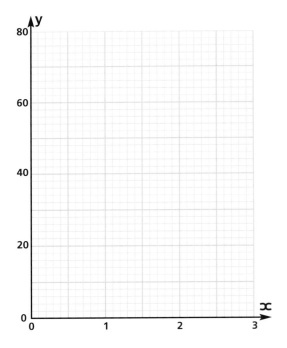

3 Draw the graphs of the following exponential functions for values of x from 0 to 4.
   a) $y = 4^x$ **b)** $y = 3 \times 0.5^x$ **c)** $y = -1 \times 2^x$

4 A graph fits the relationship $y = ab^x$. When $x = 0$, $y = 2$ and when $x = 2$, $y = 18$.
   a) Find the values of a and b and hence the relationship.
   b) Draw the graph of this relationship.

Graphs of Other Functions 3

1 **a)** Complete this table of values for the graph of $y = \sin x$.

x (°)	0	30	60	90	120	150	180	210	240	270	300	330	360
y = sin x													

b) On the grid opposite carefully plot the points and draw the graph of $y = \sin x$.

c) Use your graph to estimate two angles which have $\sin x = 0.8$

....

d) Use your graph to estimate $\sin 45°$.

....

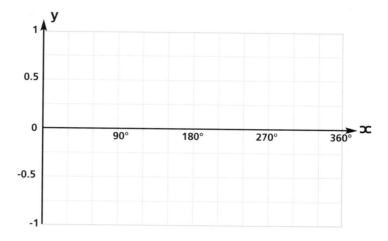

2 **a)** Complete this table of values for the graph of $y = \cos x$.

x (°)	0	30	60	90	120	150	180	210	240	270	300	330	360
y = cos x													

b) On the grid opposite carefully plot the points and draw the graph of $y = \cos x$.

c) Use your graph to estimate two angles which have $\cos x = 0.6$.

....

d) Use your graph to estimate $\cos 315°$.

....

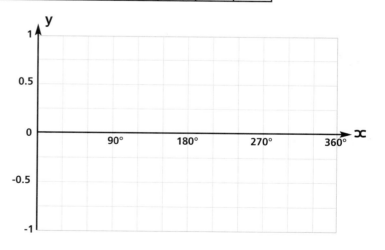

3 **a)** On a suitable grid draw the graph of $y = \tan x$ for values of x from 0° to 360°.
   b) In which ways is the graph of $y = \tan x$ similar and different to the graphs of $y = \sin x$ and $y = \cos x$.

Transformations of Functions 1

1 a) On the axes opposite draw and label the graph of $y = x^2$ for values of x from -3 to 3.

b) On the same axes, sketch and label the graphs of ...

i) $y = x^2 - 4$.

ii) $y = 3x^2$.

c) i) Describe carefully the transformation that maps $y = x^2$ onto $y = x^2 - 4$.

....

....

....

ii) Describe carefully the transformation that maps $y = x^2$ onto $y = 3x^2$.

....

....

....

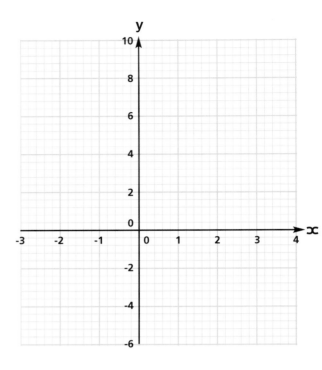

2 a) On the axes opposite draw and label the graph of $y = x^2$ for values of x from -4 to 4.

b) On the same axes, sketch and label the graphs of ...

i) $y = (x - 3)^2$.

ii) $y = (\frac{x}{3})^2$.

c) i) Describe carefully the transformation that maps $y = x^2$ onto $y = (x - 3)^2$.

....

....

....

ii) Describe carefully the transformation that maps $y = x^2$ onto $y = (\frac{x}{3})^2$.

....

....

....

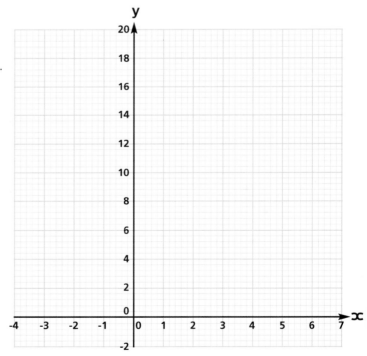

3 **Sketch these graphs on the same axes:**

a) $y = x^2$, $\quad y = 4x^2$, $\quad y = x^2 - 1$

b) $y = x^2$, $\quad y = (3x)^2$, $\quad y = (x + 5)^2$

c) $y = x^2$, $\quad y = \frac{1}{3}x^2$, $\quad y = x^2 + 3$

Transformations of Functions 2

1 a) On the same axes below sketch the graphs of **i)** $y = \sin x$ **ii)** $y = \frac{1}{2}\sin x$ and **iii)** $y = \sin 2x$.

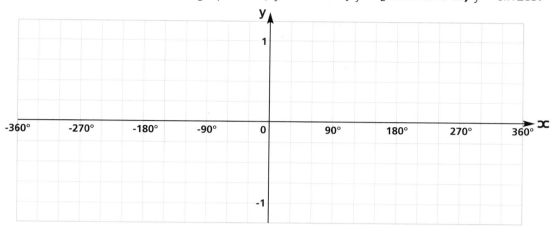

b) Describe the transformation that maps $y = \sin x$ onto ...

i) $y = \frac{1}{2}\sin x$ ....

ii) $y = \sin 2x$ ....

2 a) On the same axes below sketch the graphs of **i)** $y = \cos x$ **ii)** $y = \cos(x + 90°)$ and **iii)** $y = \cos x - 3$.

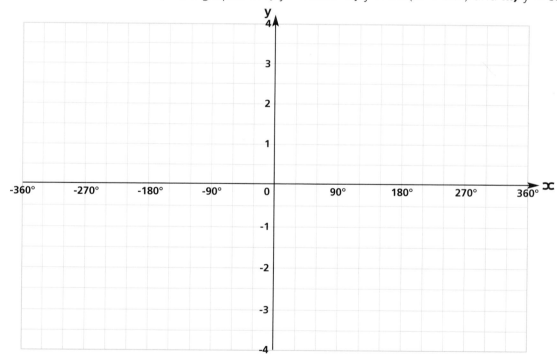

b) Describe the transformation that maps $y = \cos x$ onto ...

i) $y = \cos(x + 90°)$ ....

ii) $y = \cos x - 3$ ....

3 a) On a suitable set of axes sketch the graphs of $y = \cos x$, $y = 3\cos x$, $y = \cos x + 3$

b) On a suitable set of axes sketch the graphs of $y = \sin x$, $y = \sin\frac{1}{2}x$, $y = \sin(x + 45°)$

Other Graphs 1

1 Two towns A and B are 100 miles apart.
Mr Brown lives in A and drives to B and
Mr Smith lives in B and drives to A on the
same day, along the same route. Using
the graph opposite ...

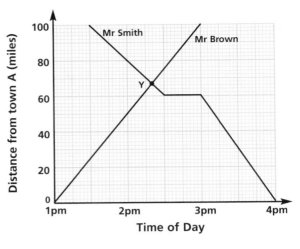

a) What time did Mr Smith set off?

....

b) Which motorist completed the journey in

the shortest time? ....

c) Who reached the highest speed and what was it? ....

d) What happened at Y? ....

e) Who stopped and for how long? ....

2 Here is part of a travel graph of Tina's
journey to the shops and back.

a) Calculate Tina's speed in km/h for the first

20 minutes. ....

....

b) Tina spends 20 minutes at the shops, then

travels back home at 48km/h.

Complete her journey on the graph.

....

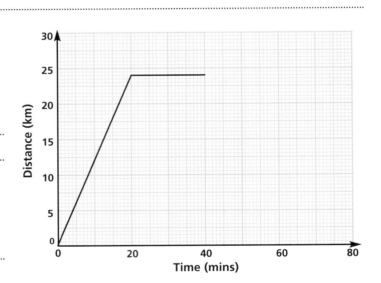

3 **a)** Plot the following data onto this velocity-time graph.

Time (s)	0	1	2	3	4	5	6
Velocity (m/s)	0	5	10	15	20	20	25

b) Calculate the acceleration of the object over the first

4 seconds.

....

....

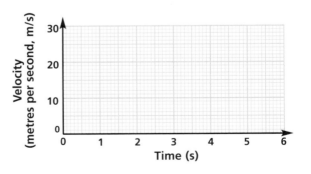

4 An object travels at a constant speed of 20m/s for the first 6 seconds, then accelerates at 5m/s² for another 4
seconds. Draw a graph to show the speed of the object over 10 seconds.

5 A train leaves town A for town B at 1pm and maintains a steady speed of 60km/h. At 2pm another train leaves
B for A maintaining a speed of 72km/h. The distance between A and B is 180km. Draw the distance-time graphs
for these trains on the same axes. When do they pass each other?

Other Graphs 2

1 **The cost of hiring a car is £30 plus an extra charge of 30p per mile.**

a) Complete this table:

Miles	0	10	20	30	50	100
Cost (£)	30	33				

b) On the axes opposite draw a graph to show the cost of hiring the car for up to 100 miles.

c) Use the graph to estimate how much it would cost to hire a car for a 52 mile journey.

....

2 **These sketch graphs show the cost of running a business over several months. Identify which sketch matches each of these descriptions.**

a) Costs are rising steadily. ....

b) Costs are falling after reaching a peak. ....

c) Costs are rising at an increasing rate. ....

d) Costs have been rising but are now levelling out. ....

3 a) If £1 = $1.4 complete the table to convert pounds sterling (£) to US dollars ($).

Pounds (£)	10	20	30	40
US Dollars ($)				

b) On the axes opposite draw the graph to convert pounds (£) to US dollars ($).

c) Use your graph to convert $30 into pounds.

....

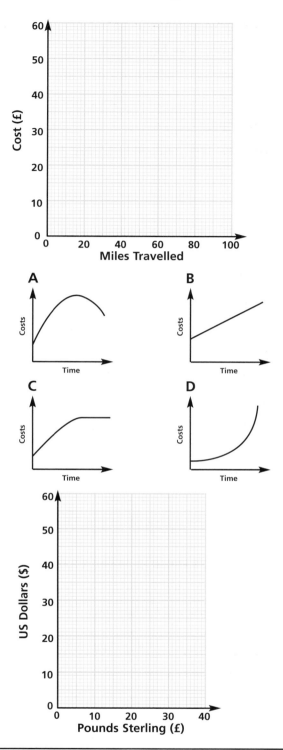

4 **Three plumbers A, B and C charge as follows: A – Call out charge £20 then £10 per hour extra.**
   B – Call out charge £30 then £5 per hour extra.   C – Standard charge £50 regardless of time.
   a) Draw a graph for each plumber's charges on the same axes, for up to 5 hours work.
   b) Which plumber is cheapest for a 30 minute job?
   c) Which plumber is cheapest for a 2½ hour job?
   d) After what time will plumber C become the cheapest?

5 **A tank of water, cuboid in shape, is being drained out at a rate of 10cm depth per minute. If the water is 60cm deep to start with, draw a graph of time against depth.**

Direct and Inverse Proportion

1 The table below gives the number of bacteria, N, in a culture at hourly intervals. The number of bacteria is directly proportional to the time, t (hours).

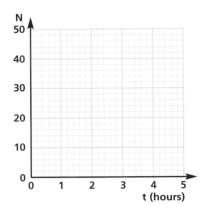

N	0	10	20	30	40	50
t (hours)	0	1	2	3	4	5

a) Draw the graph of N against t on the axes opposite.

b) What is the relationship between N and t?

....

2 The weight, W (kg), of a metal bar is directly proportional to the square of its diameter, d (cm), when the length of the bar is constant.

a) Complete the table below.

W	0	5	20	45	80	125
d	0	1	2	3	4	5
d^2	0					

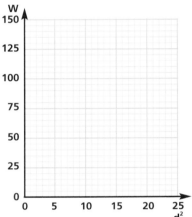

b) On the axes opposite draw the graph of W against d^2.

c) Use the graph to find the relationship between W and d.

....

3 The time, t (hours), taken to travel a given distance is inversely proportional to the average speed, s (km/hr).

a) Complete the table below.

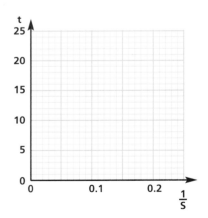

t	1	2	4	10	20
s	100	50	25	10	5
$\frac{1}{s}$					

b) Plot the graph of t against $\frac{1}{s}$.

c) What is the relationship between t and s?

....

4 The tread, t (mm), of a lorry tyre is inversely proportional to the distance travelled, d (10 000 miles). Values for t and d are given in the table.

t (mm)	10	5	2.5	1
d (10 000 miles)	1	2	4	10

a) Draw a graph of t against $\frac{1}{d}$.

b) Use the relationship between t and d to calculate the tread on a tyre after 80 000 miles.

Angles

1 For each diagram work out the sizes of angle m and angle n giving reasons for your answers. They are not drawn to scale.

a)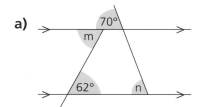

Angle m = ...

Reason: ....

....

Angle n = ...

Reason: ....

....

b)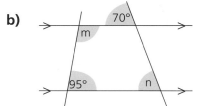

Angle m = ...

Reason: ....

....

Angle n = ...

Reason: ....

....

c)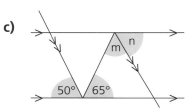

Angle m = ...

Reason: ....

....

Angle n = ...

Reason: ....

....

2 Work out the sizes of the angles marked a, b and c, giving reasons for your answers. The diagram is not drawn to scale.

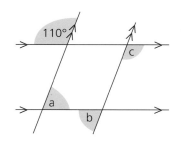

....

....

....

....

3 Work out the sizes of the angles marked p, q, r and s, giving reasons for your answers. The diagram is not drawn to scale.

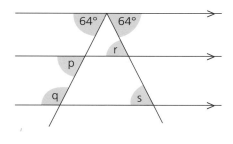

....

....

....

....

4 For each diagram work out the size of x. They are not drawn to scale.

a)

b)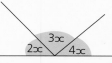

c)

d)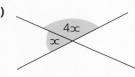

5 For each diagram work out the size of the angles marked giving reasons for your answers. They are not drawn to scale.

a)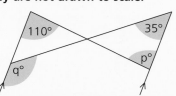

b)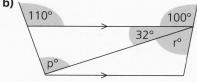

c)

Triangles

1 Draw a diagram and write a short explanation to prove that the interior angles of a triangle add up to 180°.

....
....
....
....
....

2 Draw a diagram and write a short explanation to prove that the exterior angle of a triangle is equal to the sum of the interior angles at the other two vertices.

....
....
....
....

3 This diagram has six angles marked a, b, c, d, e and f.

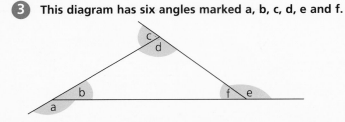

a) Work out the size of angle a in terms of angle b.

b) Work out the size of angle a in terms of angles d and f.

c) What do angles a, c and e add up to?

d) Work out the size of angle a in terms of angles c and e.

Types of Triangle

1 Below are four triangles. For each triangle work out the missing angle x and name the type of triangle giving a reason for each answer. They are not drawn to scale.

a)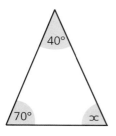

b)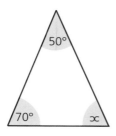

c)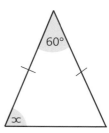

d)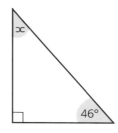

Angle x =.........................
Type of Triangle:
....
Reason:
....
....

Angle x=.........................
Type of Triangle:
....
Reason:
....
....

Angle x =.........................
Type of Triangle:
....
Reason:
....
....

Angle x =.........................
Type of Triangle:
....
Reason:
....
....

2 For each diagram below work out the size of angle p. They are not drawn to scale.

a)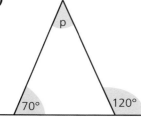

b)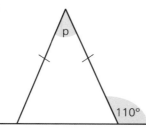

c)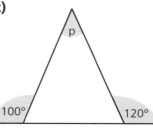

d)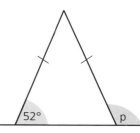

Angle p =.........................

Angle p =.........................

Angle p =.........................

Angle p =.........................

3 The diagram (not drawn to scale) shows a right-angled triangle ABC and an isosceles triangle CDE. Work out the size of the angles marked a and b giving reasons for your answers.

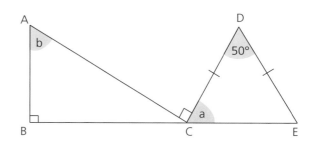

....
....

4 The diagram (not drawn to scale) shows an equilateral triangle ABC and a right-angled triangle CDE. Work out the size of the angles marked m and n giving reasons for your answers.

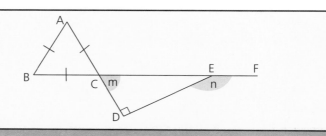

Quadrilaterals

1 Below are four quadrilaterals. For each quadrilateral work out the missing angle x and name the type of quadrilateral, giving reasons for your answers. They are not drawn to scale.

a)

b)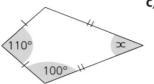

c)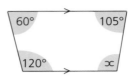

d)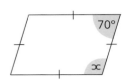

a) Angle x = ...

Type of Quadrilateral:

....

Reason:

....

....

b) Angle x = ...

Type of Quadrilateral:

....

Reason:

....

....

c) Angle x = ...

Type of Quadrilateral:

....

Reason:

....

....

d) Angle x = ...

Type of Quadrilateral:

....

Reason:

....

....

2 **Which type of quadrilateral am I?**

a) I have diagonals that are not equal in length but they bisect each other at right angles. They also bisect each of my interior angles. ....

b) I have diagonals that are equal in length and bisect each other. However, they do not bisect each other at right angles. ....

c) I have diagonals that are equal in length and bisect each other at right angles. They also bisect each of my interior angles. ....

3 **Draw a diagram and write a short explanation to prove that the interior angles of a quadrilateral add up to 360°.**

....

....

....

....

4 Calculate the size of the labelled angles in the following diagrams. They are not drawn to scale.

a)

b)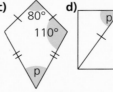

c)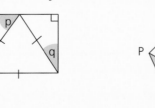

d)

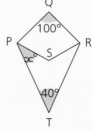

5 **a)** The interior angles of a quadrilateral are $x°$, $2x°$, $3x°$ and $4x°$. Work out the difference in size between the largest angle and the smallest angle in the quadrilateral.

b) The interior angles of a quadrilateral are $x+20°$, $x-30°$, $2x°$ and 110°. Work out the size of x.

6 **PQRS is a rhombus and PQRT is a kite. Calculate the value of x.**

Irregular & Regular Polygons

1 **For each diagram below work out the size of angle p. They are not drawn to scale.**

a)

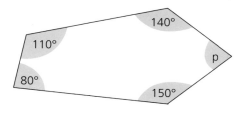

b)

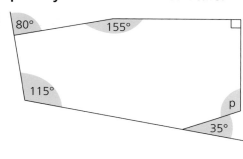

....

....

....

2 **a)** What do the exterior angles of an irregular pentagon add up to?..

b) What do the exterior angles of a regular pentagon add up to?..

3 **An irregular polygon has exterior angles equal to 110°, 94°, 88° and 68°.**

a) How many sides does the polygon have? ....

b) What is the sum of the interior angles of this irregular polygon?

....

....

4 **An irregular polygon has interior angles equal to 110°, 155°, 135°, 95°, 140° and 85°.**

a) How many sides does the polygon have? ....

b) What is the sum of the exterior angles of this irregular polygon?

....

....

5 **An irregular pentagon has four exterior angles equal to 47°, 113°, 55° and 71°. What is the size of the fifth exterior angle?**

....

....

6 **a)** How many sides does a polygon have if the sum of its interior angles is twice the sum of its exterior angles? ....

....

b) How many sides does a regular polygon have if each interior angle is equal to each exterior angle?

....

c) How many sides does a polygon have if the sum of its interior angles is equal to the sum of its exterior angles? ....

Irregular & Regular Polygons

7 A regular polygon has five sides.
Calculate the size of ...

a) each exterior angle

....

....

....

b) each interior angle.

....

....

8 A regular polygon has six sides.
Calculate the size of ...

a) each exterior angle

....

....

....

b) each interior angle.

....

....

9 The diagrams below show regular polygons, centre 0. For each polygon work out the size of the angles marked a and b.

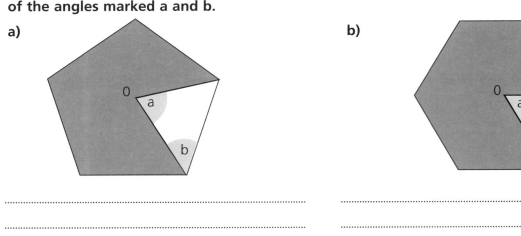

a)

....

....

....

....

b)

....

....

....

....

10 Jon reckons that it is possible to have a regular polygon where each interior angle is equal to 150° and each exterior angle is equal to 40°. Is he correct? Explain.

....

....

11 A polygon has interior angles equal to $x°$, $x + 20°$, $2x°$, $2x - 10°$ and 50°.
  a) How many sides does this polygon have?
  b) Work out the size of x.
  c) What is the size of each exterior angle?

12 A regular polygon has each interior angle equal to $1\frac{1}{2}$ times each exterior angle.
  a) What is the size of each interior angle?
  b) What is the size of each exterior angle?
  c) How many sides does this regular polygon have?

13 A regular polygon has each interior angle equal to 170°. How many sides does it have?

Congruence and Tessellation

1 Which three of these triangles are congruent? They are not drawn to scale.

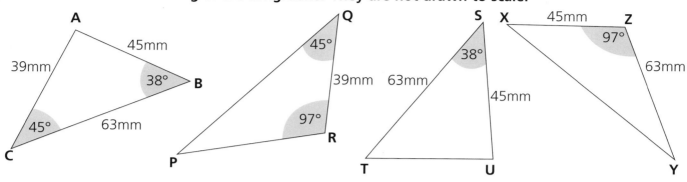

....
....

2 Which of the following pairs of triangles, A and B, are congruent? For each pair that is
congruent, give the reason why, e.g. SAS, SSS, ASA, RHS. They are not drawn to scale.

a)
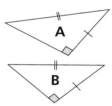

b)
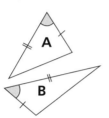

c)
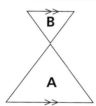

d)
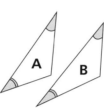

....
....

....
....

....
....

....
....

e)
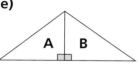

f)
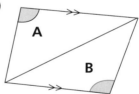

g)
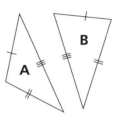

....
....

....
....

....
....

3 PQRS is a square. A and B are points on QR and SR such that QA = SB.
Use congruent triangles to prove that $P\widehat{A}Q = P\widehat{B}S$.

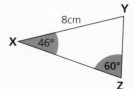

....
....

4 Here are three triangles (not drawn to scale).
Which two triangles are congruent? Explain.

5 A regular hexagon will form a tessellation
pattern but a regular pentagon does not.
Explain why.

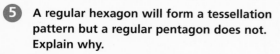

6 Using congruent triangles, prove that
the line drawn from the centre of a circle
through the midpoint of a chord is
the perpendicular bisector of the chord.

7 In the diagram PQ = ST.
Prove that triangles
PQR and RST are
congruent.

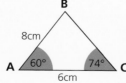

Similarity

1 **Here are four triangles (not drawn to scale).**

A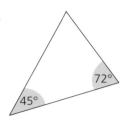

B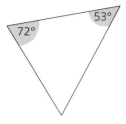

C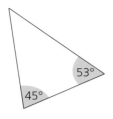

D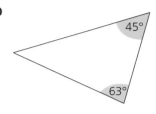

a) Pam thinks that triangles B and C are similar. Is she correct? Explain.

....

....

b) Ian thinks that triangles A and D are similar. Is he correct? Explain.

....

....

2 **These two triangles are similar. Calculate the length of...**

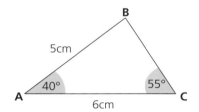

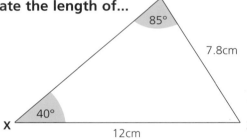

a) XY ....

b) BC ....

3 **In the diagram below BC is parallel to DE. AB = 3cm, AC = 4cm, BC = 5cm and CE = 2cm.**

The diagram is not drawn to scale.

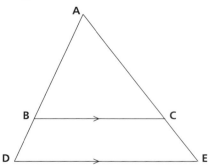

a) Calculate the length of DE.

....

....

....

b) Calculate the length of BD.

....

....

....

4 **Here are three triangles (not drawn to scale).**
Which two triangles are similar? Explain.

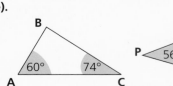

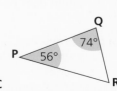

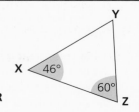

Pythagoras' Theorem 1 & 2

1 Use Pythagoras' theorem to calculate the unknown side in each of the following triangles. They are not drawn to scale. If need be, give your answer to 1 decimal place.

a)
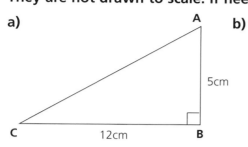

b)
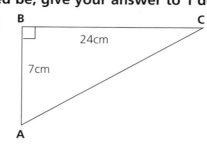

c)
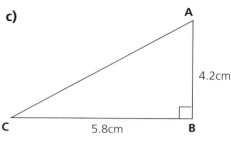

d)
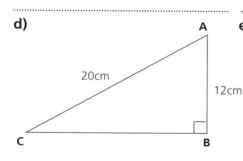

e)
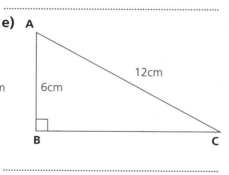

f)
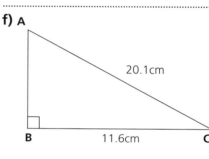

2 Which of the following triangles is not a right-angled triangle? Show all your working. They are not drawn to scale.

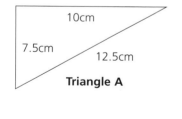

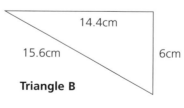

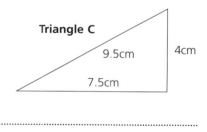

3 Calculate the height of the isosceles triangle alongside, whose sides measure 10cm, 10cm and 5cm. Give your answer to 2 significant figures. The triangle is not drawn to scale.

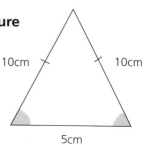

Pythagoras' Theorem 1 & 2 (cont)

4 Look at the diagram below (not drawn to scale). Use Pythagoras' theorem to calculate...

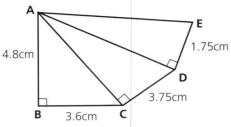

a) the length of AC.

....

....

....

....

b) the length of AE to 1 decimal place.

....

....

....

....

....

5 The diagram below shows the position of three villages (not drawn to scale). Use Pythagoras' theorem to calculate the direct distance from Lampton to Campton to 1 decimal place.

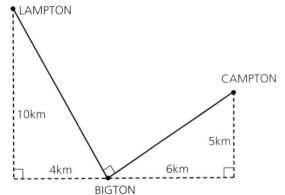

....

....

....

....

....

....

....

....

....

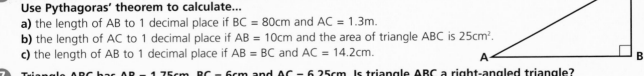

6 The diagram opposite shows a right-angled triangle ABC.
Use Pythagoras' theorem to calculate...
a) the length of AB to 1 decimal place if BC = 80cm and AC = 1.3m.
b) the length of AC to 1 decimal place if AB = 10cm and the area of triangle ABC is 25cm².
c) the length of AB to 1 decimal place if AB = BC and AC = 14.2cm.

7 Triangle ABC has AB = 1.75cm, BC = 6cm and AC = 6.25cm. Is triangle ABC a right-angled triangle? Explain your answer.

8 A square has an area of 36cm². Calculate the length of its diagonal. Leave your answer as a square root.

9 A rectangle has an area of 36cm² and the length of its base is twice that of its height.
Calculate the length of its diagonal.

10 A 4.5m ladder leans against a wall. The foot of the ladder is 1.5m from the base of the wall.
a) How high up the wall does the ladder reach? Give your answer to 1 decimal place.
b) The position of the ladder is now changed so that the distance from the foot of the ladder to the base of the wall is the same as the distance the ladder reaches up the wall. How high up the wall does the ladder now reach, to 1 decimal place?

11 The length of the diagonal of a rectangle is 12cm. The length of its base is three times that of its height.
Calculate the length of the base.

1 Use trigonometry to calculate the length of...

a) BC

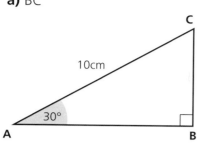

b) AB

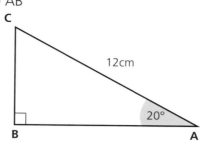

c) AB to 1 decimal place.

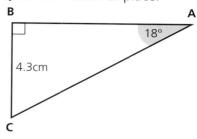

....

....

....

....

2 Use trigonometry to calculate the size of angle θ in the following triangles. If need be, give your answer to 1 decimal place.

a)

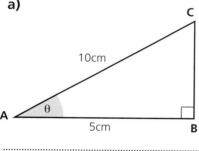

b)

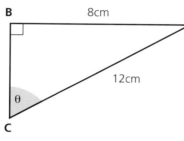

c)

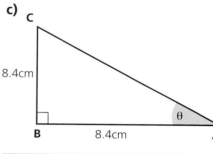

....

....

....

....

3 Which of the following triangles is right-angled? Show all your working. They are not drawn to scale.

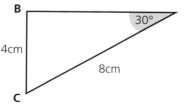

....

....

....

....

Trigonometry 1, 2 & 3 (cont)

4 The tree in the diagram is 4.2m high. From A the angle of elevation to the top of the tree is 30.4°.

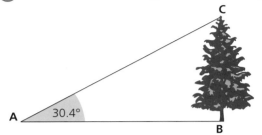

a) Calculate the distance from A to the base of the tree, B, to 1 decimal place.

....

....

....

b) The angle of elevation of the tree is now measured from a position 2m closer to the tree. Calculate the angle of elevation, to 1 decimal place.

....

....

....

5 The angle of depression from the top of one vertical pole to the top of another vertical pole is 24.5°. The height of one pole is 20m and the other is 15m. How far apart are the poles to 1 decimal place?

....

....

....

....

....

....

....

....

---

6 Triangle ABC is a right-angled triangle with BÂC = 90°. Use trigonometry to calculate...
a) Angle ABC to 1 decimal place if AB = 70cm and BC = 1.6m.
b) Angle ABC to 1 decimal place if the length of AC is twice the length of AB.
c) The length of AB to 1 decimal place if AC = 14cm and angle ACB is four times the size of angle ABC.

7 Triangle ABC has AB = 12.6cm, BC = 6.3cm and angle ACB = 60°.
Using the table of data, is triangle ABC a right angle?
Explain your answer.

Angle	sine	cosine	tangent
60°	0.866	0.5	1.732
30°	0.5	0.866	0.577

8 **a)** The angle of elevation of the top of a tower from a point 30m away from the foot of the tower is 48.2°.
Calculate the height of the tower to 1 decimal place.
b) The tower has a flag and the angle of elevation of the top of the flag from the same point is 50.4°.
Calculate the height of the flag to 1 decimal place.

9 The diagram (not drawn to scale) shows a picture hanging on a wall. AD = 3m, AB = 1.4m and CD = 1.8m.
Calculate the height and width of the picture.

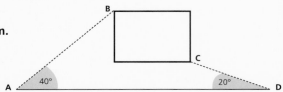

Problems Involving 3-D Figures

1 **The diagram opposite shows a cube of side 6cm.**

a) Calculate the length of AC. Give your answer
to 2 significant figures.

....

....

....

b) Calculate the length of AG. Give your answer
to 2 significant figures.

....

....

....

....

....

....

c) Calculate the size of the angle line AG makes
with the horizontal base ABCD. Give your answer
to 1 decimal place.

....

....

....

....

....

2 **The diagram opposite shows a triangular prism.**

a) Calculate the length of BC. Give your answer
to 2 significant figures.

....

....

....

b) Calculate the length of AE. Give your answer
to 2 significant figures.

....

....

....

....

....

c) Calculate the length of CE. Give your answer
to 2 significant figures.

....

....

....

....

....

d) Calculate the angle line BC makes with the
horizontal base ABED. Give your answer to
1 decimal place.

....

....

....

....

....

e) Calculate the angle line EC makes with the
horizontal base ABED. Give your answer to
1 decimal place.

....

....

....

....

....

Problems Involving 3-D Figures

3 **The diagram opposite shows a tent.**

AE = BF = DH = CG = 2.4m, AD = EH = 1.8m,

AB = EF = 1.5m and BC = FG = 1.2m.

a) Calculate the length of BE.

Give your answer to 3 significant figures.

....

....

....

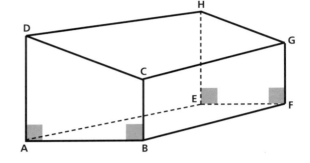

b) Calculate the length of BH.

Give your answer to 3 significant figures.

....

....

c) Calculate the length of CH.

Give your answer to 3 significant figures.

....

....

d) Calculate the angle line CH makes with the horizontal. Give your answer to 1 decimal place.

....

....

e) Calculate the angle line CD makes with the horizontal. Give your answer to 1 decimal place.

....

....

f) Calculate the angle line BH makes with the horizontal. Give your answer to 1 decimal place.

....

....

g) Calculate the total external surface area, including the base, of the tent.

....

....

4 **The diagram shows a square-base pyramid ABCDE, where AB = BC = CD = DA = 6cm and AE = BE = CE = DE = 10cm. Point E lies directly above X.**
a) Calculate the length of AC.
Give your answer to 2 significant figures.
b) Calculate the length of EX.
Give your answer to 2 significant figures.
c) Calculate the angle line AE makes with the horizontal base ABCD. Give your answer to 1 decimal place.

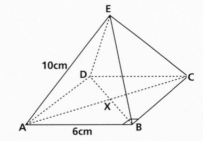

5 **The diagram shows a cuboid where AB = DC = EF = HG = 3x, BC = AD = FG = EH = 4x and AE = BF = CG = DH = √7x.**
a) Calculate the length of AC in terms of x.
b) Calculate the length of AF in terms of x.
c) Calculate the length of AG in terms of x. Leave your answer in surd form.
d) Calculate the angle line AG makes with the horizontal base ABCD. Give your answer to 1 decimal place.
e) Calculate the angle line AF makes with the horizontal base ABCD. Give your answer to 1 decimal place.

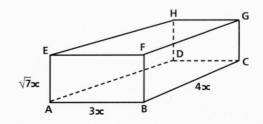

The Sine Rule & Cosine Rule

For questions 1 and 2 use the sine rule only and give your answers to 1 decimal place.
The triangles are not drawn to scale.

1 a) Calculate BC

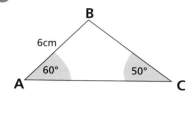

....
....
....
....

b) Calculate AB

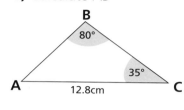

....
....
....
....

c) Calculate AC

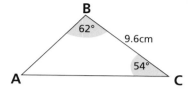

....
....
....
....

2 a) Calculate AĈB

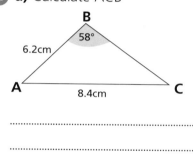

....
....
....
....
....

b) Calculate AB̂C

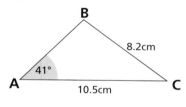

....
....
....
....
....

c) Calculate BÂC

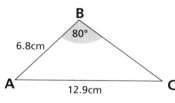

....
....
....
....
....

For questions 3 and 4 use the cosine rule only and give your answers to 1 decimal place.
The triangles are not drawn to scale.

3 a) Calculate BC

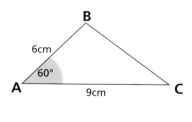

....
....
....
....
....
....

b) Calculate AC

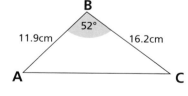

....
....
....
....
....
....

c) Calculate AB

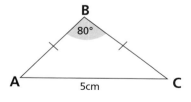

....
....
....
....
....
....

The Sine Rule & Cosine Rule

4 a) Calculate $B\hat{A}C$

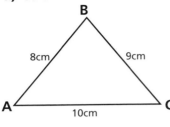

....
....
....
....
....

b) Calculate $A\hat{B}C$

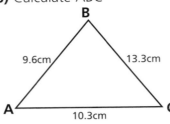

....
....
....
....
....

c) Calculate $A\hat{C}B$

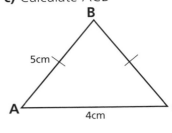

....
....
....
....
....

5 CDEF is a quadrilateral. CD = 8cm, CF = 7cm and DE = 10cm.
Angle $C\hat{D}E$ = 80° and angle $C\hat{F}E$ = 90°. Calculate the perimeter of CDEF.

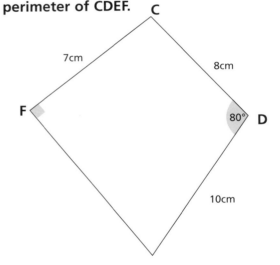

....
....
....
....
....
....
....
....
....
....

6 The direct distance from a post office, P, to a shop, S, is 100m and to a newsagent, N, is 67m. If $S\hat{N}P$ = 85°, calculate ... **a)** $P\hat{S}N$ and **b)** the distance from the shop to the newsagent. Give your answers to 1 decimal place.

7 Three girls, Alex, Bambi and Carrie, stand at three points. The bearing of Bambi from Alex is 075° and the bearing of Carrie from Alex is 143°. The distance from Alex to Bambi is 165m and the distance from Alex to Carrie is 192m. Calculate ...
a) the distance from Bambi to Carrie
b) the bearing of Carrie from Bambi
c) the bearing of Bambi from Carrie. Give your answers to 1 decimal place.

8 The diagram shows the end wall of a house. If the distance from B to D is 6.9m, calculate **a)** $B\hat{C}D$ **b)** $C\hat{B}D$ **c)** the distance AE and **d)** the area of the end wall section of the house. Give your answers to 1 decimal place.

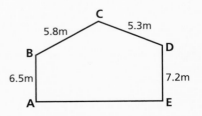

1 The grid shows twelve shapes A to L.

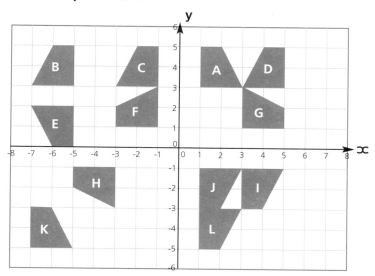

a) Give the letter of the image which is object A reflected...

i) in the x-axis .... **ii)** in the y-axis... **iii)** in the line $x = 3$.............................

iv) in the line y = 1................................. **v)** in the line y = x................................. **vi)** in the line y = $-x$.............................

b) Describe the single reflection which takes B to E. ....

c) Describe the single reflection which takes F to G. ....

2 Triangles A, B, C and D are all different reflections of the green triangle. For each one draw in the mirror line and describe the reflection fully.

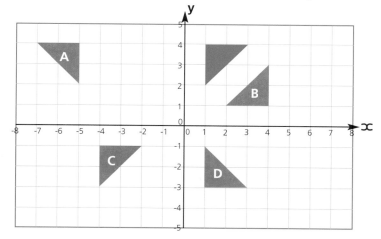

Triangle A: ....

....

Triangle B: ....

....

Triangle C: ....

....

Triangle D: ....

....

3 **A is a triangle with coordinates (3,1), (5,1) and (5,2).**
   a) On a suitable grid draw triangle A.
   b) i) Reflect triangle A in the line $x = 1$. Label this triangle B. **ii)** Reflect triangle A in the line y = -1. Label this triangle C.
   iii) Reflect triangle A in the line y = x. Label this triangle D. **iv)** Reflect triangle A in the line y = $-x$. Label this triangle E.

Transformations 2

1 **The grid shows ten shapes A to J.**

a) Give the letter of the image which is object A rotated...

i) 90° clockwise about the origin (0,0)

....

ii) 180° clockwise about the origin (0,0)

....

iii) 270° clockwise about the origin (0,0)

....

iv) 90° clockwise about the centre (-2,0)

....

v) 180° clockwise about the centre (-1,1)

....

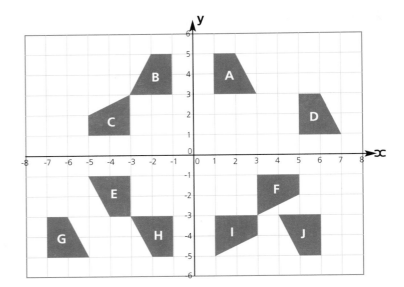

b) Describe the single rotation which takes C to A. ....

c) Describe the single rotation which takes I to A. ....

2 **The grid shows triangle A.**

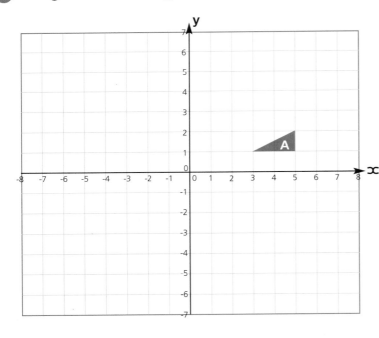

a) Rotate triangle A 90° clockwise about the origin (0,0). Label this triangle B.

b) Rotate triangle A 180° clockwise about the origin (0,0). Label this triangle C.

c) Rotate triangle A 270° clockwise about the origin (0,0). Label this triangle D.

d) Rotate triangle A 90° clockwise about the centre (3,1). Label this triangle E.

e) Rotate triangle A 270° clockwise about the centre (-1,1). Label this triangle F.

3 **A is a quadrilateral with coordinates (2,2), (4,4), (5,3) and (5,1).**

a) On a suitable grid draw quadrilateral A.

b) i) Rotate quadrilateral A 90° clockwise about the origin (0,0). Label this quadrilateral B. ii) Rotate quadrilateral A 180° clockwise about the origin (0,0). Label this quadrilateral C. iii) Rotate quadrilateral A 270° clockwise about the origin (0,0). Label this quadrilateral D. iv) Rotate quadrilateral A 90° clockwise about the centre (2,2). Label this quadrilateral E.

v) Rotate quadrilateral A 180° clockwise about the centre (-1,-1). Label this quadrilateral F.

Transformations 3

1 **The grid shows ten shapes A to J.**

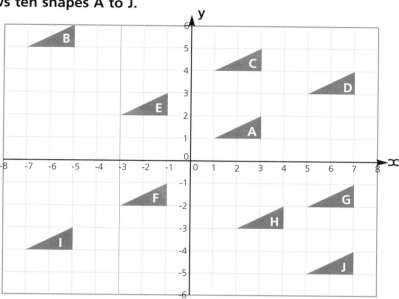

a) Give the letter of the triangle which is shape A translated by the vector ...

i) $\begin{pmatrix} 4 \\ 2 \end{pmatrix}$ ....

ii) $\begin{pmatrix} 1 \\ -4 \end{pmatrix}$ ....

iii) $\begin{pmatrix} -4 \\ 1 \end{pmatrix}$ ....

iv) $\begin{pmatrix} 0 \\ 3 \end{pmatrix}$ ....

v) $\begin{pmatrix} -8 \\ -5 \end{pmatrix}$ ....

vi) $\begin{pmatrix} 4 \\ -6 \end{pmatrix}$ ....

b) What is the translation vector which maps triangle D onto triangle A?.................................

c) What is the translation vector which maps triangle B onto triangle A? ....

2 **The grid shows triangle A. Draw and label the following translations:**

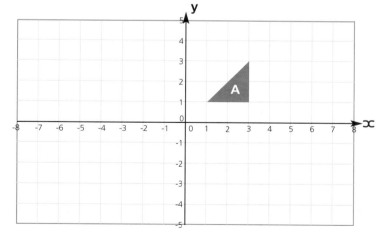

a) Triangle A mapped onto triangle B by the translation vector $\begin{pmatrix} 4 \\ 2 \end{pmatrix}$

b) Triangle A mapped onto triangle C by the translation vector $\begin{pmatrix} -5 \\ -4 \end{pmatrix}$

c) Triangle A mapped onto triangle D by the translation vector $\begin{pmatrix} -8 \\ 0 \end{pmatrix}$

d) Triangle A mapped onto triangle E by the translation vector $\begin{pmatrix} 5 \\ -6 \end{pmatrix}$

3 **A is a triangle with coordinates (-1,-3), (-3,-2) and (-4,4).**

a) On a suitable grid draw triangle A.

b) i) Translate triangle A by the vector $\begin{pmatrix} 5 \\ 5 \end{pmatrix}$ Label this triangle B. **ii)** Translate triangle A by the vector $\begin{pmatrix} -5 \\ -5 \end{pmatrix}$ Label this triangle C.

iii) Translate triangle A by the vector $\begin{pmatrix} 5 \\ -5 \end{pmatrix}$ Label this triangle D. **iv)** Translate triangle A by the vector $\begin{pmatrix} -5 \\ 5 \end{pmatrix}$ Label this triangle E.

Transformations 4

1 **The grid shows triangle A.**

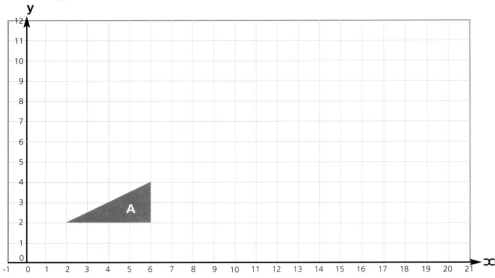

Enlarge triangle A by...

a) a scale factor of 3 about the centre of enlargement (0,0). Label this triangle B.

b) a scale factor of 2 about the centre of enlargement (0,3). Label this triangle C.

c) a scale factor of ½ about the centre of enlargement (0,0). Label this triangle D.

d) a scale factor of 2 about the centre of enlargement (4,0). Label this triangle E.

2 **The grid shows three quadrilaterals A, B and C.**

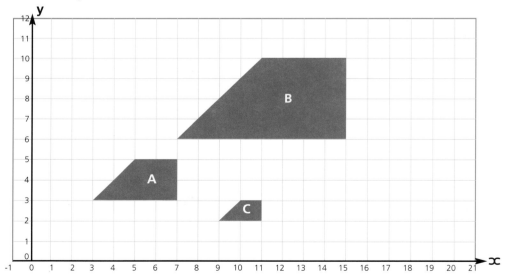

Describe fully the enlargement that would map quadrilateral A...

a) onto B ....

b) onto C ....

3 **Triangle A has coordinates (3,2), (6,2) and (6,4).** **a)** On a suitable grid draw triangle A.
   b) Complete the following enlargements:
   i) Triangle A is enlarged by a scale factor of 2, centre of enlargement (0,0). Label this triangle B.
   ii) Triangle A is enlarged by a scale factor of ½, centre of enlargement (0,0). Label this triangle C.
   iii) Triangle A is enlarged by a scale factor of 3, centre of enlargement (1,1). Label this triangle D.

1 **On the axes below, draw the enlargement of triangle ABC by ...**

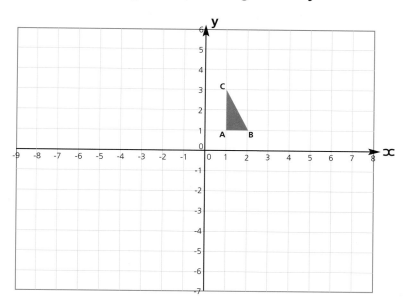

i) scale factor -2, centre (0,0). Label this triangle A'B'C'.

ii) scale factor -3, centre (0,1). Label this triangle A"B"C".

iii) scale factor -½, centre (1,0). Label this triangle A'''B'''C'''.

2 **Describe fully the transformation that maps triangle P onto ...**

i) Q ....

ii) R ....

iii) S ....

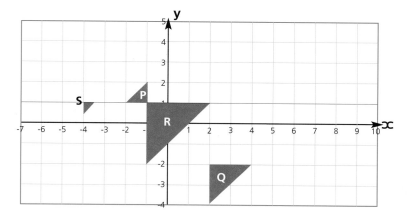

3 **Triangle A has coordinates (-1,1), (-3,1) and (-3,3).**
   a) Using an x-axis and y-axis from -10 to 10, draw triangle A.
   b) Enlarge triangle A by **i)** scale factor -3, centre (0,0). This is triangle B. **ii)** scale factor -½, centre (0,1). This is triangle C.
   c) i) Describe fully the transformation that maps triangle B onto triangle A.
   ii) Describe fully the transformation that maps triangle C onto triangle A.

Transformations 6

1 **The grid shows three triangles A, B and C.**

a) Describe fully a single transformation that would map triangle A onto...

i) triangle B ....

ii) triangle C ....

b) Describe fully a single transformation that would map triangle B onto triangle C.

....

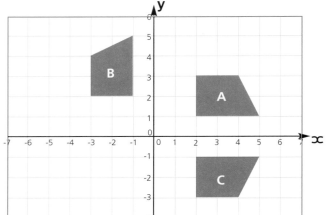

2 **The grid shows three quadrilaterals A, B and C.**

a) Describe fully a single transformation that would map quadrilateral A onto...

i) quadrilateral B ....

ii) quadrilateral C ....

b) Describe fully a single transformation that would map quadrilateral B onto quadrilateral C.

....

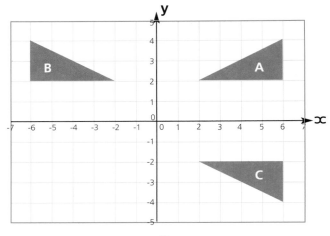

3 **The grid shows triangle A.**

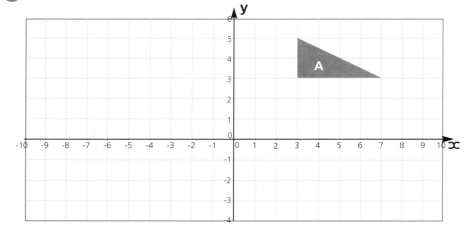

a) Triangle A is reflected in the line $x = 1$. Draw and label this triangle B.

b) Triangle A is reflected in the line y = 1. Draw and label this triangle C.

c) Describe fully the single transformation that would map triangle B onto triangle C.

....

....

4 a) Quadrilateral A has coordinates (3,3), (6,3), (7,6) and (5,6). On a suitable grid draw quadrilateral A.

b) Quadrilateral A is reflected in the line $x = 2$. Draw and label quadrilateral B.

c) Quadrilateral A is reflected in the line y = 0. Draw and label quadrilateral C.

d) Quadrilateral A is rotated 270° clockwise about the origin (0,0). Draw and label quadrilateral D.

e) Describe fully the single transformation that would map quadrilateral B onto quadrilateral C.

f) Describe fully the single transformation that would map quadrilateral D onto quadrilateral C.

Coordinates 1

1 Write down the coordinates of the letters A to H on the graph opposite.

A ....
B ....
C ....
D ....

E ....
F ....
G ....
H ....

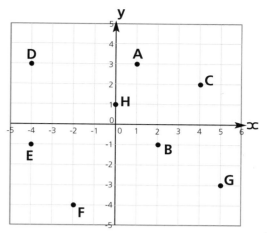

2 Write down the coordinates of each of the vertices (corners) of this box, apart from (0,0,0).

A ....
B ....
C ....
D ....

E ....
F ....
G ....

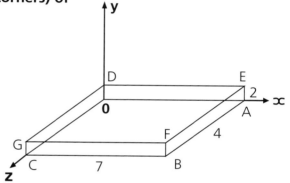

3 This cube has a side length of 5cm.

a) Write down the coordinates of each of the vertices, apart from (0,0,0).

A ....
B ....
C ....
D ....

E ....
F ....
G ....

b) What are the coordinates of the point of intersection of the two diagonals 0B and AC?

....

c) What are the coordinates of the point of intersection of the two diagonals 0F and AG?

....

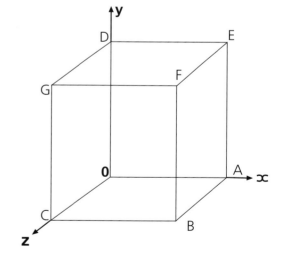

4 Draw axes from -5 to 5 on the x-axis and -3 to 4 on the y-axis.
  a) Draw and label A (4,2), B (-5,2), C (-4,-2) **b)** Draw and label a fourth coordinate D to produce a parallelogram ABCD.

5 The four base coordinates of a cube are (0,0,0), (3,0,0), (3,3,0) and (0,3,0).
  Draw a 3-D graph and write down the other 4 coordinates.

Coordinates 2

1 **a)** On the graph opposite, plot the coordinates
A (1,2), B (3,5), C (7,6) and D (7,3).

b) Find the coordinates of the midpoint, M,
of the line segments ...

i) AB ....

....

ii) BC ....

....

iii) CD ....

....

iv) AD ....

....

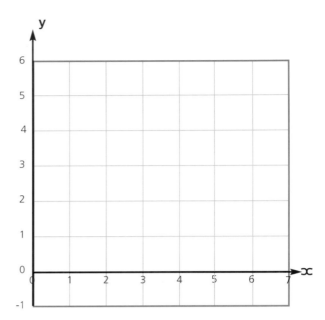

2 **a)** On the graph opposite, plot the coordinates
P (3,1), Q (0,3), R (4,6), S (7,4).

b) Calculate the lengths of the line segments ...

i) PQ ....

....

....

....

....

ii) QR ....

....

....

....

....

iii) RS ....

....

....

....

....

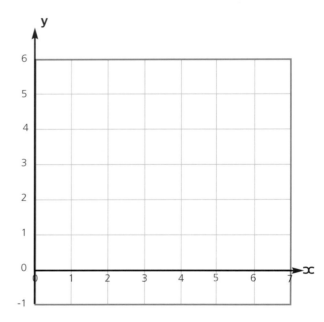

iv) SP ....

....

....

....

....

---

3 The line segment AB has coordinates (-2,-1) and (6,4) respectively. Find the coordinates of the midpoint M.

4 Hexagon ABCDEF has coordinates A (-2,3), B (2,3), C (4,0), D (2,-4), E (-2,-4), F (-4,0).
  a) Plot these on a graph to produce a hexagon.
  b) Find the coordinates of the midpoint, M, for line segments **i)** AF **ii)** BC **iii)** CD **iv)** EF.
  c) Calculate the lengths of the line segments and hence find the perimeter of the hexagon (to 1 d.p.).

1 The diagram below shows eight different vectors.

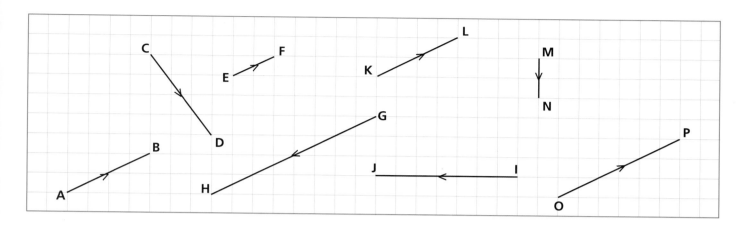

a) Write all the vectors in the diagram in the form $\begin{pmatrix} x \\ y \end{pmatrix}$.

$\overrightarrow{AB} = \begin{pmatrix} \ \end{pmatrix}$, $\overrightarrow{CD} = \begin{pmatrix} \ \end{pmatrix}$, $\overrightarrow{EF} = \begin{pmatrix} \ \end{pmatrix}$, $\overrightarrow{GH} = \begin{pmatrix} \ \end{pmatrix}$, $\overrightarrow{IJ} = \begin{pmatrix} \ \end{pmatrix}$, $\overrightarrow{KL} = \begin{pmatrix} \ \end{pmatrix}$, $\overrightarrow{MN} = \begin{pmatrix} \ \end{pmatrix}$, $\overrightarrow{OP} = \begin{pmatrix} \ \end{pmatrix}$

b) What is the relationship between...

i) $\overrightarrow{AB}$ and $\overrightarrow{KL}$? ....

ii) $\overrightarrow{AB}$ and $\overrightarrow{EF}$? ....

iii) $\overrightarrow{AB}$ and $\overrightarrow{GH}$? ....

iv) $\overrightarrow{AB}$ and $\overrightarrow{OP}$? ....

c) Complete the following. Give your answers in the form $\begin{pmatrix} x \\ y \end{pmatrix}$.

i) $\overrightarrow{AB} + \overrightarrow{CD}$

ii) $\overrightarrow{AB} - \overrightarrow{CD}$

iii) $\overrightarrow{HG} + \overrightarrow{EF}$

iv) $\overrightarrow{HG} - \overrightarrow{GH}$

v) $\overrightarrow{IJ} + \overrightarrow{OP}$

vi) $2\overrightarrow{KL} + \overrightarrow{GH}$

vii) $\overrightarrow{IJ} + \overrightarrow{MN}$

viii) $\frac{1}{2}\overrightarrow{GH} - \overrightarrow{KL}$

ix) $\overrightarrow{OP} - \overrightarrow{PO}$

x) $\overrightarrow{AB} + \overrightarrow{CD} + \overrightarrow{MN}$

Vectors 1 & 2 (cont)

2 The diagram below shows three vectors a, b and c.

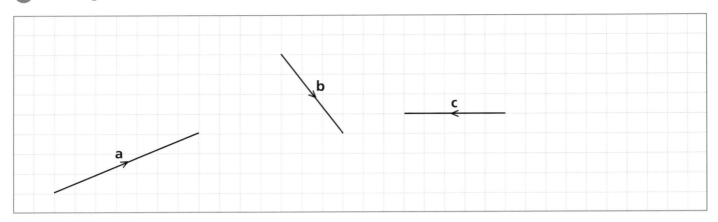

On the grid below, draw and label diagrams to represent...

a) a + b   **b)** a - b   **c)** b + c   **d)** b - c   **e)** 2a - c   **f)** a - 3c

3 If a = $\begin{pmatrix} 3 \\ 4 \end{pmatrix}$, b = $\begin{pmatrix} 2 \\ 3 \end{pmatrix}$, c = $\begin{pmatrix} -4 \\ -3 \end{pmatrix}$ and d = $\begin{pmatrix} 4 \\ -1 \end{pmatrix}$, on a suitable grid draw diagrams to represent...

a) 2a   **b)** 2c   **c)** a + b   **d)** a + c   **e)** b + c   **f)** b – c   **g)** c – d   **h)** c + 2d

Vector Geometry

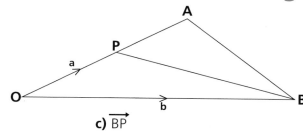

1 OAB is a triangle. P is the midpoint of OA. $\overrightarrow{OA}$ = a and $\overrightarrow{OB}$ = b. Express the following vectors in terms of a and/or b:

a) $\overrightarrow{AB}$

....

....

b) $\overrightarrow{PA}$

....

....

c) $\overrightarrow{BP}$

....

....

2 OABC is a rectangle. P and Q are the midpoints of AB and OC respectively. $\overrightarrow{OA}$ = a and $\overrightarrow{OC}$ = c.

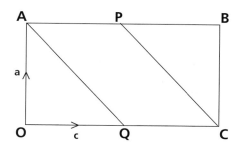

a) Express the following vectors in terms of a and/or c.

i) $\overrightarrow{CB}$ ....   **ii)** $\overrightarrow{AB}$ ....

iii) $\overrightarrow{PB}$ ....   **iv)** $\overrightarrow{OQ}$ ....

v) $\overrightarrow{PC}$ ....

vi) $\overrightarrow{AQ}$ ....

b) What can you deduce about shape APCQ? Explain your answer.

....

....

3 OABC is a parallelogram. P is a point on OA so that OP = $\frac{1}{3}$OA, Q is a point on OC so that OQ = $\frac{1}{3}$OC, X is a point on AB so that AX = $\frac{1}{3}$ AB and Y is a point on CB so that CY = $\frac{1}{3}$CB. $\overrightarrow{OA}$ = a and $\overrightarrow{OC}$ = c.

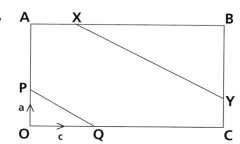

a) Express the following vectors in terms of a and/or c:

i) $\overrightarrow{OP}$ ....   **ii)** $\overrightarrow{OQ}$ ....

iii) $\overrightarrow{PQ}$ ....   **iv)** $\overrightarrow{BX}$ ....

v) $\overrightarrow{BY}$ ....   **vi)** $\overrightarrow{XY}$ ....

b) What can you deduce about shape PXYQ? Explain your answer.

....

....

....

4 P, Q, R and S are the midpoints of sides AB, BC, CD and DA of parallelogram ABCD respectively. Prove that PQRS is also a parallelogram.

5 G and H are the midpoints of sides AB and AC of triangle ABC respectively.
 a) Prove that triangles AGH and ABC are similar.
 b) What is the ratio of the two triangles' areas?

Circumference of a Circle

1 A window is in the shape of a semicircle on top of a rectangle, as shown in the diagram. If AB = 1.8m and BC = 90cm, calculate the perimeter of the window to 1 decimal place. Take π = 3.14.

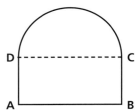

....
....
....
....

2 Mrs Jones' garden is rectangular. At each end there is a semicircular flower bed and the rest of the garden is lawn, as shown in the diagram. If AB = 10m and BC = 8m, calculate the perimeter of the lawn. Take π = 3.14.

....
....
....
....

3 A company makes cone-shaped containers using card shaped as in diagram A. The finished cone is made by bringing the straight edges together as in diagram B.

Diagram A

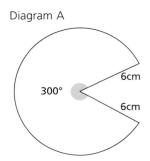

a) Find the arc length of the card in diagram A.
Give your answer in terms of **π.**

....
....
....

b) Calculate the radius of the base of the cone in diagram B.

Diagram B

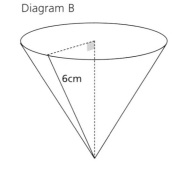

....
....
....

---

4 Calculate the circumference of the following circles to 1 decimal place. Take π = 3.14.
   a) Radius = 12cm **b)** Radius = 1.2cm **c)** Diameter = 12cm **d)** Diameter = 120cm

5 Sector OAB (shaded) is cut out of a circle with a radius of 16cm.
   a) Calculate the perimeter of sector OAB.
   b) Calculate the perimeter of the major sector left over.

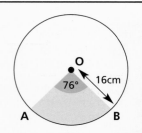

1 Calculate the area of the following shapes (π = 3.14).

a)
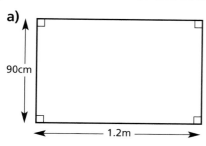

b)
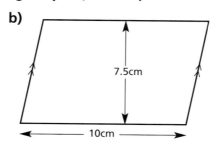

c)
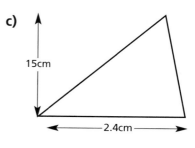

....

....

d)
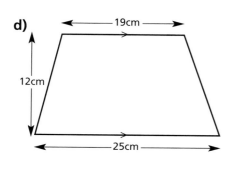

e)
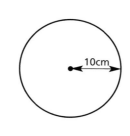

f)
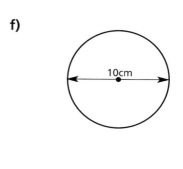

....

....

2 A circular table has an area of **11.304m²**.
Calculate its radius to 1 d.p. Take π = 3.14.

....

....

....

....

3 A circular flower bed has an area of **7.065m²**.
Calculate its radius to 1 d.p. Take π = 3.14.

....

....

....

....

4 Calculate the area of the following shape
to 1 d.p. It is not drawn to scale (π = 3.14).

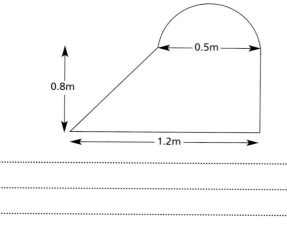

....

....

....

....

5 Calculate the area of the minor sector OAB.
Take π = 3.14. The diagram is not drawn
to scale.

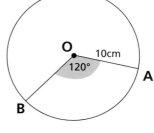

....

....

....

....

Area 1 & 2 (cont)

6 Calculate the areas of these triangles to 2 decimal places.

a)

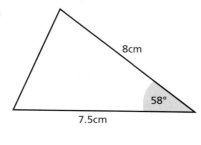

8cm

58°

7.5cm

b)

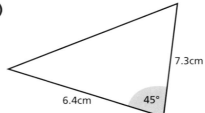

7.3cm

6.4cm   45°

c)

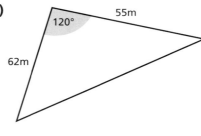

55m

120°

62m

....

....

....

....

7 The diagram opposite shows a field. Calculate its area.

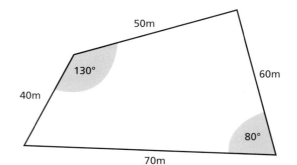

50m

130°

40m

60m

80°

70m

....

....

....

....

....

8

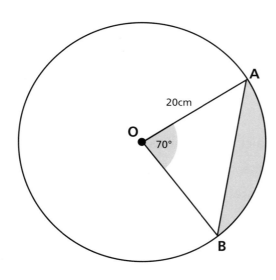

A

20cm

O

70°

B

a) Calculate the area of triangle OAB to 2 decimal places.

....

....

....

....

b) Calculate the area of sector OAB. Hence, find the area of the shaded segment to 2 decimal places.

....

....

....

....

9 Calculate the area of the following triangles:
   a) Triangle ABC has AB = 38cm, BC = 25cm and $A\hat{B}C$ = 58°.
   b) Triangle ABC has AB = 20cm, BC = 5cm and $A\hat{B}C$ = 100°.

1 Calculate the surface area of the following solids to 1 d.p.

a)

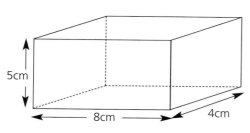

b)

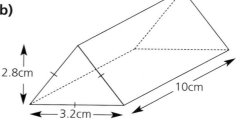

....

....

....

....

....

....

....

....

2 The outside of a cylindrical drum is painted. The drum has a radius of 5cm and a height of 12cm. $\pi = 3.14$. Find the total surface area of the drum including both ends, to 3 s.f.

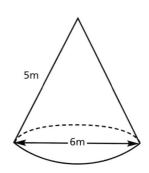

....

....

....

....

3 A child's night light is spherical in shape, with radius 4cm. Calculate the surface area of the light to 3 s.f. ($\pi = 3.14$).

....

....

4 Calculate the total surface area of the cone-shaped tent opposite. Take $\pi = 3.14$.

....

....

....

5 A property developer decides to varnish the floorboards in the living room of one of his houses. A plan of the floor is shown alongside. It is not to scale. One tin of varnish will cover 16m² and costs £4.99. If he wants to apply two coats of varnish to the whole floor, how much will it cost him?

6 Using $\pi = 3.14$, calculate the surface area of a sphere with...
a) radius 7cm. b) radius 3.7cm. c) diameter 10cm. d) diameter 28cm.

Volume 1 & 2

1 **Calculate the volume of the following solids.**

a)

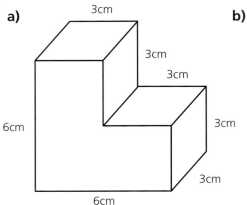

b)

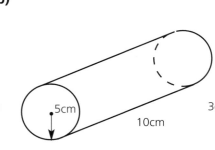

$\pi = 3.14$

c)

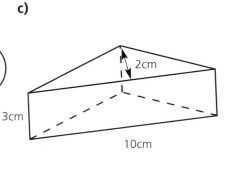

....

....

....

....

2 **a)** The following cylinder has a volume of 314cm³.
Calculate the missing length represented by x
($\pi = 3.14$).

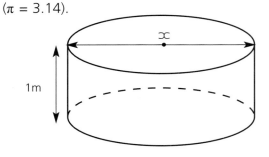

b) The following solid has a volume of 100cm³.
Calculate the missing length represented by x.

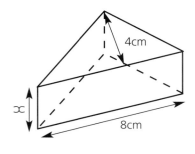

....

....

....

....

3 **A water tank is 40cm by 24cm by 14cm. It contains
water to a depth of 8cm. Six identical spheres are
placed in the tank and fully submerged. The
water level rises by 3.5cm.
Calculate the radius of the spheres.**

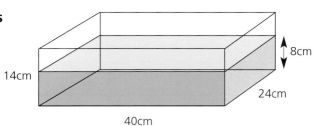

....

....

....

....

Volume 1 & 2 (cont)

4 A child's toy is made of a hollow cylinder with a hollow cone on top. The toy has enough water to just fill the cylinder. The toy is turned upside down. Calculate the depth of water, x.

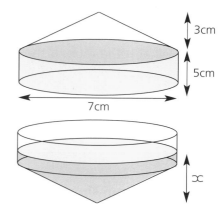

....

....

....

....

....

5 The tank opposite contains water. The depth of the water is 50cm. All the water is poured into a cylindrical tank which has a diameter of 44cm. Calculate the depth of the water in the cylindrical tank (to 1 d.p.) $\pi = 3.14$.

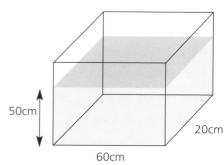

....

....

....

....

....

6 In the following expressions the letters r and h represent length. π, 2, 3, 4, 5, and 10 are numbers which have no dimension. Write down whether each of the following expressions represent perimeter, area, volume or none of them.

a) $r(\pi + 2)$ ....

b) $\dfrac{4r^2\pi}{h}$ ....

c) $r(r + 4h)$ ....

d) $\dfrac{rh}{4}$ ....

e) $10r^3\pi$ ....

f) $\pi(r + 2h)$ ....

g) $\dfrac{3r^3}{h}$ ....

h) $r^2(h + \pi r)$ ....

---

7 A cylindrical mug has internal radius 5cm and internal height 8cm.
a) Calculate the volume of liquid it can hold (to 3 significant figures) ($\pi = 3.14$).
b) If 500cm³ of liquid is poured into the mug, what depth of liquid would be in the mug?

8 If x and y both represent length, which of the following expressions represents i) length, ii) area, iii) volume?

$\dfrac{x}{y}$, $\sqrt{x^3}$, $x^2 + y^2$, $\dfrac{x^2}{y}$, xy^2, x^2y^2, $x^2 + y^3$

Lonsdale REVISION GUIDES   Revision Guide Reference: Page 100 & 101   **SHAPE, SPACE & MEASURES**   **97**

Similar Figures

1 Two figures are similar. The ratio of two corresponding lengths is 2:3.

  a) What is the ratio of their areas? ....

  b) What is the ratio of their volumes? ....

2 Two figures are similar. The ratio of their areas is 6.25:16. What is the ratio of their volumes?

....

....

3 The diagram shows two similar figures, Figure A and Figure B. The height of Figure A is 12cm and the height of Figure B is 27cm.

Figure B

Figure A

12cm

27cm

  a) If the surface area of Figure A is 72cm², calculate the surface area of Figure B.

....

....

....

....

....

  b) If the volume of Figure B is 243cm³, calculate the volume of Figure A.

....

....

....

....

....

4 Two figures are similar. The volume of Figure A is 108cm³ and the volume of Figure B is 500cm³. If the surface area of Figure B is 60cm², what is the surface area of Figure A?

....

....

....

5 Two figures are similar. The surface area of Figure A is 150cm² and the surface area of Figure B is 294cm². If the volume of Figure A is 275cm³, what is the volume of Figure B?

....

....

....

6 Three bottles are similar. Bottle A has a height of 6cm, a surface area of 12cm² and a volume of 9cm³.
  a) If Bottle B has a surface area of 75cm², calculate ... **i)** its height and **ii)** its volume.
  b) If Bottle C has a volume of 72cm³, calculate ... **i)** its height and **ii)** its surface area.

7 Is it possible for Figure A, which has a height of 22cm and a volume of 135cm³, to be similar to Figure B which has a height of 33cm and a volume of 320cm³? Explain.

3-D Shapes 1 & 2

1 **a)** What shape is the base of the cuboid shown opposite?

....

b) Which edges are equal in length to CD?

....

c) Which lengths equal AH?

....

d) How many vertices does the cuboid have?

....

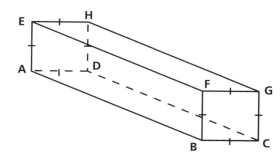

2 **An equilateral triangular prism has a tetrahedron placed on top of it. For this combined solid...**

a) How many edges does it have? ....

b) How many vertices? ....

c) How many faces? ....

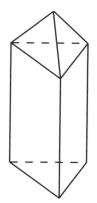

3 **On the grid below draw full-size diagrams of the following solids:**

a)

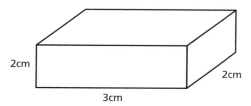

2cm

2cm

3cm

b)

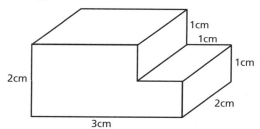

1cm
1cm
1cm
2cm
2cm
2cm
3cm

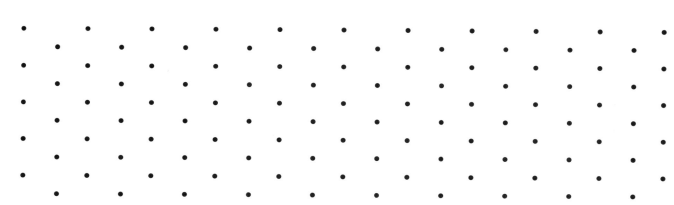

4 **Draw a sketch of the plan view of this square-based pyramid.**

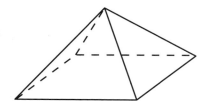

3-D Shapes 1 & 2 (cont)

5 The diagram alongside shows a solid. Draw and label an accurate diagram of the solid showing...

a) plan view **b)** front elevation **c)** side elevation

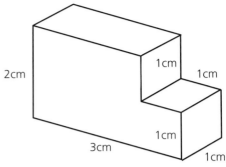

6 A net of a solid is shown opposite.

a) What is the name of the 3-D solid?

....

b) How many vertices does it have?

....

c) Which other corners meet at D? Put an X on each one.

d) How many planes of symmetry does the solid have?

....

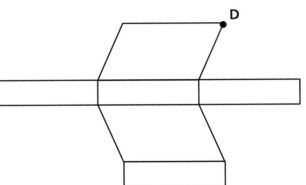

7 Which of the following are nets for a triangular prism? Place a tick beside the correct net(s).

a)

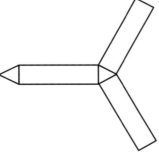

b)

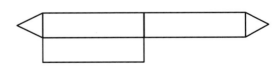

c)

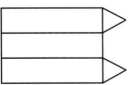

d)

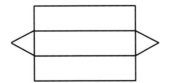

8 Draw an accurate full-size net of a regular hexagonal prism if each edge is 3cm long.

9 How many planes of symmetry does a cube have?

10 For the solid shown opposite, draw the ...
a) plan **b)** front elevation **c)** side elevation.

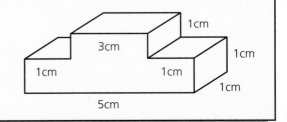

Symmetry 1 & 2

1 Draw all the lines of symmetry for each of the following shapes.

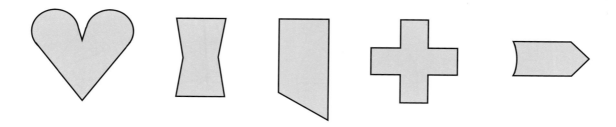

2 Mark on the lines of symmetry for each of these letters.

M S H B Z A V C K

3 How many lines of symmetry does each of the following quadrilaterals have?

a) Square .... □

b) Rectangle .... ▭

c) Parallelogram .... ▱

d) Rhombus .... ◇

e) Kite .... ◁

f) Trapezium .... ◿

4 For each of the following shapes draw in all the lines of symmetry and also write down the order of rotational symmetry for each shape.

a)

b)

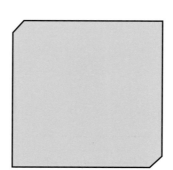

c)

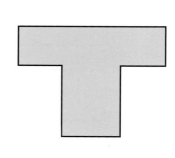

Order of rotational symmetry:

....

Order of rotational symmetry:

....

Order of rotational symmetry:

....

5 **What is the order of rotational symmetry for each of these shapes?**

a)

b)

c)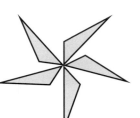

d)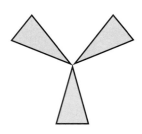

Order: ....   Order: ....   Order: ....   Order: ....

6 **a)** Draw accurately a regular pentagon with sides 3cm long and interior angles 108°.

b) Mark on the lines of symmetry.

c) What is the order of rotational symmetry?

....

7 **a)** Draw a regular hexagon. Interior angles are 120°.
   b) Draw in all lines of symmetry and write down the order of rotational symmetry.

8 **Write down the order of rotational symmetry for each of the following quadrilaterals:**
   a) Square **b)** Rectangle **c)** Parallelogram **d)** Rhombus **e)** Kite **f)** Trapezium.

Scale Drawings & Map Scales

1 a) Draw an accurate scale drawing of this garden using a scale of 1cm to represent 2.5m.

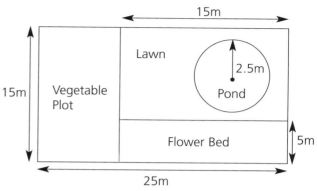

b) What is the actual diagonal distance across the garden in metres?

....

2 This is part of a map of Devon and Cornwall drawn to a scale of 1cm : 10km.

a) What is the direct distance from Launceston to Exeter?

....

....

b) What is the direct distance between Bodmin and Looe?

....

....

c) Which three places are a direct distance of 43km from Tavistock?

....

....

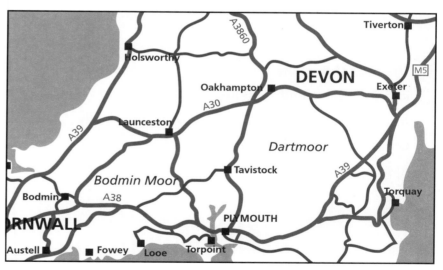

3 Draw an accurate scale drawing of a rectangular field 80m long and 50m wide. By measurement find the actual distance diagonally, from one corner to the opposite corner, to the nearest metre.

4 The diagram alongside shows a sketch of one side of a house.
   a) Draw an accurate scale drawing using a scale of 1cm to 1m.
   b) By measurement, find the actual height of the house (x).

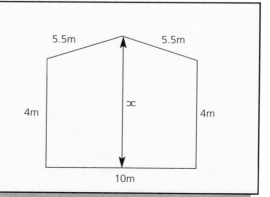

Measuring Bearings

1 The diagram shows the position of the coastguard (C), the beach (B) and a yacht (Y).

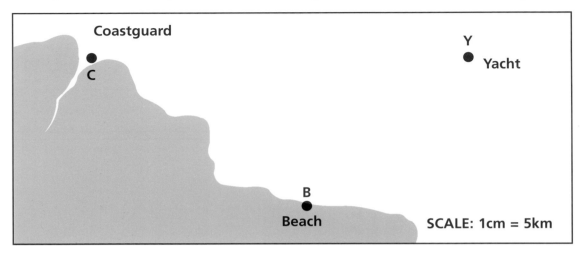

Coastguard

Y
Yacht

C

B
Beach

SCALE: 1cm = 5km

a) What is the bearing of...

i) Y from C? .... **ii)** Y from B? ....

iii) B from C? .... **iv)** B from Y? ....

v) C from Y? .... **vi)** C from B? ....

b) What is the actual distance from...

i) C to B? .... **ii)** C to Y? .... **iii)** B to Y? ....

2 The map shows the position of four towns A, B, C and D on an island. A helicopter flies directly from A to B, then B to C, then C to D and finally D back to A. On what four bearings must it fly?

A → B ....

B → C ....

C → D ....

D → A ....

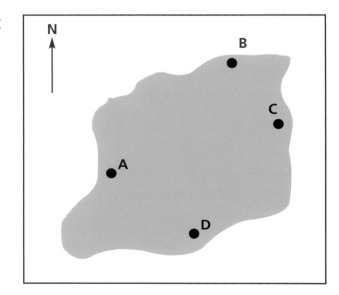

N

B

C

A

D

3 An explorer walks 1 000m on a bearing of 070° and then walks 2 000m on a bearing of 160°.
a) Draw an accurate scale drawing of his route.
b) By measurement, find the bearing he must follow to return directly to his starting point.

4 Treasure is buried on an island according to the following instructions:
"The treasure lies on a bearing of 100° from the coconut tree and on a bearing of 200° from the cactus plant. The cactus plant is 20m due east of the coconut tree."
Draw a scale drawing using 1cm to 5m to show the position of the treasure.

Converting Measurements

1 Convert...

a) 450cm into metres

....

....

b) 3.5 litres into millilitres

....

c) 1.25kg into grams

....

d) 6 874g into kilograms

....

....

e) 45km into metres

....

....

f) 0.55cm into millimetres

....

....

2 Convert these lengths into metres.

a) 1 005cm

....

....

b) 1.937km

....

....

c) 2 650mm

....

....

3 Put these weights into order of size, starting with the smallest.

420g, 4kg, 39.5kg, 4 220mg, 0.405kg

....

....

....

4 Convert...

a) 45cm into inches

....

....

b) 6 ounces into grams

....

....

c) 5 gallons into litres

....

....

5 Terry is 1.5m tall. Jake is 68 inches tall. Who is the taller and by how much?

....

....

....

---

6 Put the following lengths into decreasing order of size:
1km, 900m, 1 200m, 11 000cm, 1 050 000mm

7 Convert...
a) 3 miles into kilometres **b)** 12km into miles **c)** 4.5 pounds into grams **d)** 360g into pounds **e)** 12 pints into litres
f) 22.5 litres into pints

8 Sue ran a 10km race. How many yards did she run altogether? (1760 yards = 1 mile).

Compound Measures

1 Work out the time taken to travel 92km at an average speed of 55km/h.

....

....

2 A marathon runner completed 26.2 miles in a course record of 2hrs 20mins.
What was his average speed?

....

....

3 A tortoise took 20 minutes to get from one end of the garden to the other. His average speed is 2cm per second. How long is the garden in metres?

....

....

....

4 A boat travels for $2\frac{1}{2}$ hours at 100km/h and then $1\frac{1}{2}$ hours at 80km/h. Calculate its average speed for the whole journey.

....

....

....

5 A cylindrical tree stump weighs 15kg.
Its dimensions are shown opposite.
Calculate the density of the wood.

....

....

....

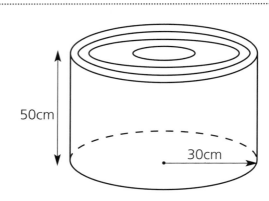

50cm

30cm

6 Water has a density of 1g/cm^3 and ice has a density of 0.9g/cm^3.
450cm^3 of water is frozen. By how much does the volume of the water change when it freezes?

....

....

....

7 **a)** Change 30 metres per second into kilometres per hour.
b) A car travels 30 metres per second for $3\frac{1}{2}$ hours. How far does it travel in kilometres?

8 **The density of oak wood is 800kg per m^3.**
a) Change this to g per cm^3.
b) How much does a solid oak table top measuring 110cm by 80cm by 5cm weigh?

Constructions 1 & 2

1 Construct a triangle ABC with sides AB = 4cm, BC = 3cm and angle ABC = 40°.

2 On your triangle ABC in question 1 above, construct the bisector of angle BAC.

3 **a)** Construct a triangle PQR where PQ is 6cm, QR is 5cm and PR is 2cm.

   b) Construct the perpendicular bisector of PQ and where this line meets QR, label it S.

4 The sketch opposite shows three towns A, B and C. B is on a bearing of 040° from A. C is due East of A and B is on a bearing of 300° from C. C is 40km from A. Construct an accurate scale drawing.

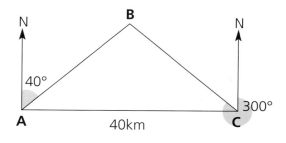

5 Showing all construction lines, and by using a pair of compasses and a ruler, construct the perpendicular bisector of each side of this equilateral triangle.

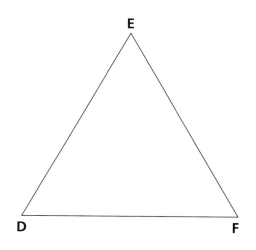

Constructions 1 & 2 (cont)

6 **Using the line AB below as a starting point, use a pair of compasses and a ruler to...**

a) Construct a 90° angle at A.

b) Construct a 90° angle at B.

c) Complete the construction to make a square.

A _____ B

7 **In the space below draw a triangle XYZ.**

a) Construct the bisectors of the three angles $\hat{X}$, $\hat{Y}$ and $\hat{Z}$.

b) What do you notice? ....

8 Using only a ruler and a pair of compasses, construct an equilateral triangle of side 3cm and a square of side 6cm.

9 Construct the following triangles using a ruler and a pair of compasses.

a)

7.4cm   5.3cm

5.3cm

b)

6.2cm

60°

7.3cm

c)

8.4cm

60°

9cm

d)

6.5cm

5.5cm

1 The map below shows three trees, A, B and C, in a park. Along one edge of the park there is a straight path. Treasure is buried in the park. The treasure is: nearer to C than A, more than 150m from the path and between 100m and 200m from B. Using a ruler and compass only, shade the region where the treasure must be buried. You must show all construction lines.

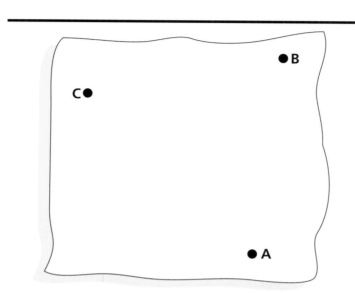

path

Scale 1cm : 50m

2 A goat is tethered by a rope 4m long to a rail PQ 8m long. The rope can move along the rail from P to Q. Draw an accurate diagram of the locus of points showing the boundaries of the area where the goat can graze.

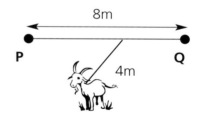

3 Draw a triangle ABC where AB = 7cm, BC = 9cm, B̂ = 90°.
  a) Draw the locus of points inside the triangle which are equidistant from A and B.
  b) Draw the locus of points inside the triangle which are equidistant from B and C.
  c) Find and label a point, D, which is equidistant from A and B and equidistant from B and C.

4 Draw the same triangle ABC as for question 3.
  a) Draw the locus of points equidistant from line AB and AC.
  b) A point (P) moves inside triangle ABC, equidistant from AB and AC and greater than 6cm away from C. Show the locus of points where P can move.

5 **a)** Draw the graph of the set of points which are equidistant from the x and y axes.
  b) What is the equation of the graph?
  c) On the same axes draw the graph of the set of points where the y coordinate is twice the x coordinate.
  d) What is the equation of this graph?

Properties of Circles 1

1 Name each of the parts of the circle labelled A to F opposite.

a) A ....
b) B ....
c) C ....
d) D ....
e) E ....
f) F ....

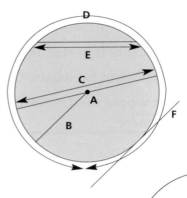

2 In the diagram opposite, O is the centre of the circle. AB is a tangent touching the circle at C. OC = AC. Find the size of...

a) angle COA ....

b) angle ODC ....

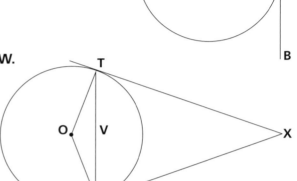

3 XT and XW are tangents touching the circle at T and W.

a) Draw the axis of symmetry in OTXW.

b) Name three pairs of congruent triangles.

....

c) If angle TXW is 40° what is angle TOW?

....

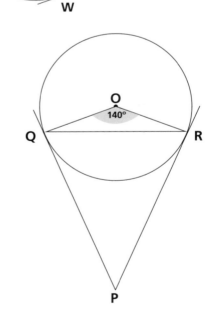

4 In the diagram opposite, O is the centre of the circle and PQ and PR are tangents.

a) What name is given to triangle OQR? ....

b) Find the size of angle...

i) OQR ....

ii) ORQ ....

c) Find the size of angle...

i) RQP ....

ii) QRP ....

iii) QPR ....

d) What type of triangle is PQR? ....

5 a) In diagram A calculate the length OX if the chord is 10m long and radius OW is 8m long.

b) In diagram B, AB and CD are parallel chords. OPQ is perpendicular to AB and CD. Explain why AC = BD.

Diagram A

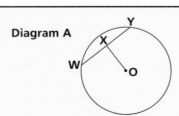

Diagram B

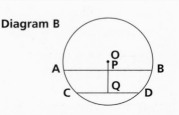

Properties of Circles 2 & 3

1 Find the size of x. Give a reason for each answer. The diagrams are not drawn to scale.

a)

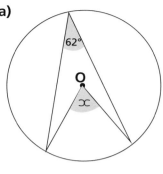

....
....

b)

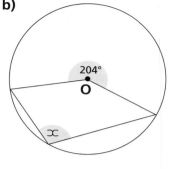

....
....

c)

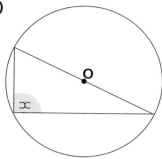

....
....

d)

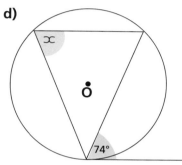

....
....

e)

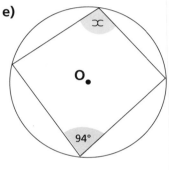

....
....

f)

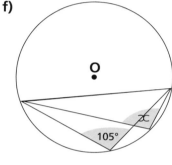

....
....

g)

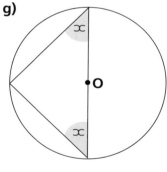

....
....

h)

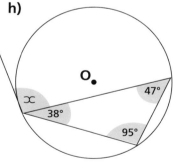

....
....

i)

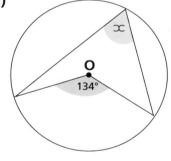

....
....

j)

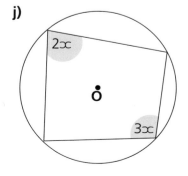

....
....

k)

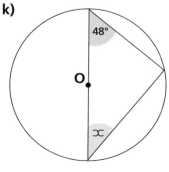

....
....

l)

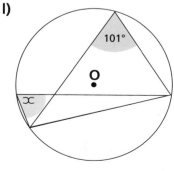

....
....

2 Find the sizes of x and y. Give reasons for your answers. The diagrams are not drawn to scale.

a)

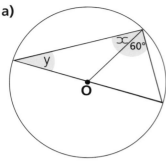

b)

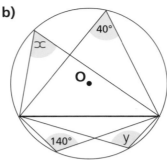

c)

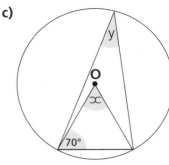

....

....

....

....

....

....

3 Find the size of angle AED in each diagram. Give a reason for each answer. They are not drawn to scale.

a)

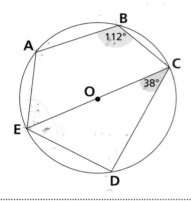

b)

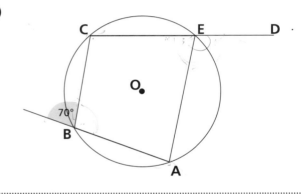

....

....

....

....

4 PQRS is a cyclic quadrilateral. BPA is a tangent to the circle at P. PS is parallel to QR, RQ = RS.
Find the size of angle $\widehat{SPQ}$.

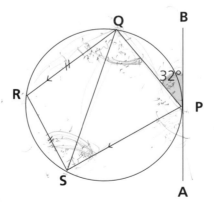

....

....

....

....

....

....

5 By means of a suitable diagram prove the following:
a) The angle subtended by a semicircle is 90°. **b)** Opposite angles of a cyclic quadrilateral add up to 180°.
c) The angle subtended between a tangent to a circle and its chord is equal to the angle subtended in the alternate segment. **d)** Angles subtended by an arc are equal in size. **e)** Angles subtended in the same segment are equal in size.

1 **Tim has ten cards (shown below). They are placed face down and mixed up.**

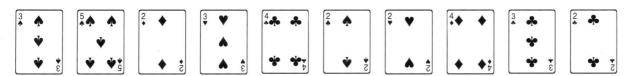

a) What is the probability that a card picked at random will be...

i) a 2? .... **ii)** a 3? .... **iii)** a 4? ....

iv) a 5? .... **v)** not a 2? .... **vi)** not a 3? ....

b) Here is a probability scale:

On the scale above ....

i) mark with an A the probability that a card picked at random will be a 2.

ii) mark with a B the probability that a card picked at random will be a 3.

iii) mark with a C the probability that a card picked at random will be a 4.

iv) mark with a D the probability that a card picked at random will be a 5.

2 **An ordinary six-sided die is biased. The probabilities of the die landing on each number are shown in the table. Work out the value of p.**

....

....

....

....

Number	1	2	3	4	5	6
Probability	p	$\frac{1}{6}$	$\frac{1}{6}$	$\frac{1}{6}$	$\frac{1}{6}$	$\frac{5}{18}$

3 **Jack has the following spinner. He spins it.**

a) What is the probability that the spinner does not land on a 1?

....

b) What is the probability that the spinner does not land on a 2?

....

c) What is the probability that the spinner lands on a 3?

....

4 A box contains 7 red balls and 3 blue balls. A ball is picked out at random. What is the probability that it is ...
a) red? **b)** not red? **c)** blue? **d)** not blue? **e)** red or blue? **f)** black?

5 A kitchen cupboard contains tins of baked beans, peas, carrots and potatoes only. The probability of picking a tin of potatoes is $\frac{1}{12}$, while the probability of picking a tin of carrots is three times that of a tin of potatoes, and a tin of peas is twice that of a tin of carrots.
a) What is the probability of picking ... **i)** a tin of carrots? **ii)** a tin of peas? **iii)** a tin of baked beans?
b) What is the probability of not picking ... **i)** a tin of carrots? **ii)** a tin of peas? **iii)** a tin of baked beans?
c) If the cupboard contains 4 tins of baked beans, how many tins are there in the cupboard altogether?

Probability 2

1 There are a number of red, white and blue beads in a bag. The probability of picking a red bead is $\frac{1}{3}$ and the probability of picking a blue bead is $\frac{1}{5}$.

a) What is the probability of picking a red or blue bead?

....

b) What is the probability of picking a white or red bead?

....

....

2 There are 52 cards in a pack. One is picked at random. What is the probability that it is ...

a) a heart or a diamond? ....

b) a heart or a king? (Careful!) ....

3 If two dice are thrown, what is the probability of the results being ...

a) two sixes? ....

b) two odd numbers? ....

4 There are 10 discs in a bag, of which 3 are blue. Two discs are picked out at random without being replaced. What is the probability of getting two blue discs?

....

....

5 Vicky has a set of five cards, shown below. They are placed face down. She also has an ordinary die.

A card is picked at random and the die is thrown.

a) What is the probability of throwing a 3 or 4 with the die and picking up a card with a 2 on it?

....

b) What is the probability of throwing an odd number with the die and picking a card with an odd number on it?

....

---

6 A box contains 3 blue, 4 yellow, 5 red and 2 green sweets. One is taken out and eaten. A second is then taken out. What is the probability that ...
a) both sweets are green? **b)** both sweets are the same colour?

7 The probability of being stopped by traffic lights at a certain set of roadworks is 0.7.
Suzie drives the same route every day for 3 days. What is the probability she will be stopped two times over the next 3 days?

Listing all Outcomes

1 **Two dice are thrown and the two numbers are added together to give a total score.**

a) Complete the sample space diagram below to show all the scores.

<table>
<tr><td rowspan="2"></td><td rowspan="2"></td><td colspan="6">First Die</td></tr>
<tr><td>+</td><td>1</td><td>2</td><td>3</td><td>4</td><td>5</td><td>6</td></tr>
<tr><td rowspan="6">Second Die</td><td>1</td><td>2</td><td>3</td><td>4</td><td></td><td></td><td></td></tr>
<tr><td>2</td><td>3</td><td>4</td><td></td><td></td><td></td><td></td></tr>
<tr><td>3</td><td>4</td><td></td><td></td><td></td><td></td><td></td></tr>
<tr><td>4</td><td></td><td></td><td></td><td></td><td></td><td></td></tr>
<tr><td>5</td><td></td><td></td><td></td><td></td><td></td><td></td></tr>
<tr><td>6</td><td></td><td></td><td></td><td></td><td></td><td></td></tr>
</table>

b) What is the probability that the total score will be ...

i) equal to 7? ....

ii) greater than 7?...

iii) a prime number?..

iv) a square number? ....

v) greater than 12?..

vi) a multiple of 3? ....

vii) a factor of 12? ....

2 **Francis has the following coins in her pocket:**

Jim has the following coins in his pocket:

Two coins are picked out at random, one from Francis' pocket and one from Jim's pocket.

The values of the two coins are added together to give a total.

a) Complete the sample space diagram below to show all the values.

<table>
<tr><td rowspan="2"></td><td colspan="7">Francis' Coin</td></tr>
<tr><td></td><td></td><td></td><td></td><td></td><td></td><td></td></tr>
<tr><td rowspan="7">Jim's Coin</td><td></td><td></td><td></td><td></td><td></td><td></td><td></td></tr>
<tr><td></td><td></td><td></td><td></td><td></td><td></td><td></td></tr>
<tr><td></td><td></td><td></td><td></td><td></td><td></td><td></td></tr>
<tr><td></td><td></td><td></td><td></td><td></td><td></td><td></td></tr>
<tr><td></td><td></td><td></td><td></td><td></td><td></td><td></td></tr>
<tr><td></td><td></td><td></td><td></td><td></td><td></td><td></td></tr>
<tr><td></td><td></td><td></td><td></td><td></td><td></td><td></td></tr>
</table>

b) What is the probability that the total value of the two coins added together is ...

i) equal to 6p?...

ii) equal to 11p? ....

iii) less than 10p?..

iv) greater than 40p?..

v) less than 40p?..

vi) equal to 40p? ....

3 **Bruce has an ordinary die. Robin has the spinner shown alongside:**
The spinner is spun and the die is thrown to give two numbers.
  a) Draw a sample space diagram to show all the possible scores if the numbers are multiplied together.
  b) What is the probability that the score is ... **i)** equal to 12? **ii)** equal to 24? **iii)** a multiple of 10?
    iv) a factor of 4? **v)** an odd number? **vi)** an even number?

Tree Diagrams 1 & 2

1 The probability that Steve arrives at school on time on any particular day is 0.7.

a) Complete the tree diagram for two school days, Monday and Tuesday.

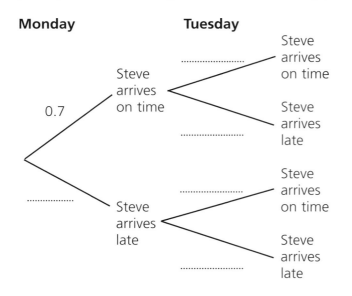

Monday **Tuesday**

0.7 — Steve arrives on time
.... — Steve arrives on time
.... — Steve arrives late

.... — Steve arrives late
.... — Steve arrives on time
.... — Steve arrives late

b) What is the probability that ...

i) Steve arrives on time on Monday and Tuesday?

....

ii) Steve arrives late on Monday and Tuesday?

....

iii) Steve arrives late on Monday only?

....

iv) Steve arrives late on Tuesday only?

....

v) Steve arrives late on one day only?

....

2 Vicky, Donna and Petra are going to have two races. The probability that Vicky wins either of the two races is 0.5, while the probability that Donna wins either of the two races is 0.3.

a) What is the probability of Petra winning either of the two races? ....

b) Complete the tree diagram.

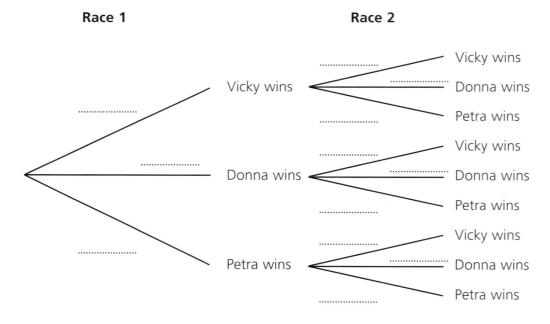

Race 1 **Race 2**

Vicky wins
.... — Vicky wins
.... — Donna wins
.... — Petra wins

Donna wins
.... — Vicky wins
.... — Donna wins
.... — Petra wins

Petra wins
.... — Vicky wins
.... — Donna wins
.... — Petra wins

c) What is the probability that...

i) Vicky wins both races? ....

ii) Vicky does not win a race? ....

iii) Donna wins Race 1 and Petra wins Race 2? ....

iv) Race 1 and Race 2 are won by different girls? ....

Tree Diagrams 1 & 2 (cont)

3 A bag contains 12 counters of which 6 are black, 4 are white and 2 are red. A counter is picked out at random and, without it being replaced, another counter is picked out at random.

a) In the space below draw a tree diagram to show all the different possible outcomes.

b) What is the probability that ...

i) Both counters picked out are the same colour? ....

ii) Both counters picked out are different colours? ....

iii) Neither of the counters picked out are black? ....

---

4 The probability that Julie does her school homework on any particular day is 0.8.
a) Draw a tree diagram to show all the probabilities for two days.
b) Using the tree diagram, what is the probability that Julie ... **i)** does her homework on both days? **ii)** does her homework on one day only? **iii)** does not do her homework on either day?

5 Rolf is a cricketer. The probability that Rolf's team win a game is $\frac{1}{2}$ and lose is $\frac{1}{3}$. They can also draw. Rolf's team have a cricket game on Saturday and another game on Sunday.
a) Draw a tree diagram to show all the probabilities. b) Using the tree diagram, what is the probability that Rolf's team
i) wins both games? **ii)** wins on Saturday only? **iii)** wins one game only? **iv)** does not lose either game?

6 A bag contains 12 balls of which 4 are red, 3 are blue, 3 are green and 2 are yellow. A ball is picked out at random and, without it being replaced, another ball is picked out at random.
a) Draw a tree diagram to show all the different possible outcomes.
b) What is the probability that ... **i)** both balls are the same colour? **ii)** both balls are different colours? **iii)** neither of the balls picked out is red?

Relative Frequency

1 **The following spinner is spun 120 times:**

a) How many times would you expect the

spinner to land on ...

i) a 1? .... **ii)** a 2? .... **iii)** a 3? ....

b) The actual number of times the spinner landed on a 1, 2 and 3 is shown in the table below. For each

number calculate the relative frequency.

Number	Number of times landed	Relative Frequency
1	66	....
2	38	....
3	16	....

2 **Jane tosses a coin 50, 100, 150, 200**

and 250 times. She records the

number of tails she gets in a table

(shown alongside).

a) Complete the table by calculating

the missing relative frequencies.

b) On the grid below draw a bar

graph to show the relative frequency

of the coin landing on tails.

c) If Jane kept tossing the coin,

what would you expect the relative

frequency of the coin landing on tails

to become? Explain why.

....

....

....

....

....

Number of tosses	Number of tails	Relative Frequency
50	20	0.4
100	44	....
150	80	....
200	92	....
250	120	....

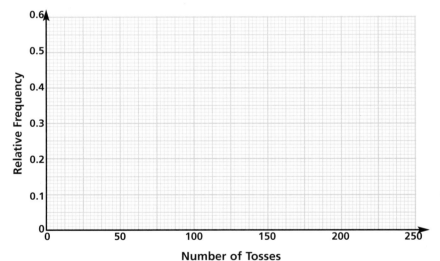

3 **Below are the results of an experiment where a die was thrown and the number of 6s was recorded.**

Number of throws	30	60	90	120	150	180	210	240	270	300	330	360
Number of 6s thrown	3	5	10	16	23	28	35	42	47	49	52	59
Relative frequency												

a) Complete the table by calculating the missing relative frequencies.

b) Draw a bar graph to show the relative frequency of throwing a 6.

c) How many 6s would you expect to be thrown if the experiment was continued and the die was thrown 1500 times?

Collecting Data 1 & 2

1 **What is the difference between primary data and secondary data?**

....

....

....

2 **a)** What is sampling?

....

b) What is the difference between a random sample and a stratified sample?

....

....

c) A recent survey carried out in Manchester suggests that 90% of the national population prefer football to rugby. The survey was conducted on 200 males. Has this survey provided reliable data? Explain why.

....

....

....

3 **a)** State two conditions that must be satisfied when collecting data for a stratified sample.

Condition 1 ....

Condition 2 ....

b) A small village has a population of 350 as shown in the table.

Age (years)	0 -12	13 -24	25 - 40	41 -60	61+
No. of people	33	48	107	92	70

A stratified sample of 50 is planned. Calculate the number of people that should be sampled from each group.

....

....

....

....

....

....

....

Collecting Data 1 & 2 (cont)

④ Joe works in a supermarket. He decides to use a questionnaire to find out about the shopping habits of the customers who come into the store. Here is the first question:
'How old are you? Tick the correct box'.

10 years and under		11 years to 20 years		21 years to 40 years		41 years to 60 years		61 years to 80 years		80 years and over	

a) Make up two more suitable questions Joe could use for his questionnaire.

....

....

b) Make up two questions which would not be suitable for his questionnaire.

....

....

⑤ In a survey a group of pupils were asked, 'How long did you spend watching TV over the weekend?'

a) Design a suitable observation sheet to collect this information.

b) How would you make sure that the information obtained was from a random sample?

....

....

---

⑥ Molly works in a pizza parlour. She decides to use a questionnaire to find out about the eating habits of the people who come into the parlour.
    a) Make up three suitable questions Molly could use for her questionnaire.
    b) Make up three questions which are not suitable for her questionnaire.

⑦ Jimmy is carrying out a survey to investigate what the pupils in his school spend their pocket money on.
    a) Design a suitable observation sheet for him to collect the information.
    b) How could Jimmy make sure that the information collected was random?

1 **What is the difference between discrete and continuous data?**

....

....

....

....

2 **Jane is carrying out a traffic survey. She records the number of cars that pass her house every 30 seconds for a period of 20 minutes. Group her data by completing the frequency table below.**

Number of cars

4 3 4 X 2 5 5 4 3 2
4 5 3 2 4 4 4 5 5 X
2 4 3 5 4 3 3 5 2 4
2 4 3 5 2 X X 4 5 3

Number of cars	Tally	Frequency
1	IIII	4
2		
3		
4		
5		

3 **A survey was carried out on the number of residents in each house on a street.**

The results are given below:

4 , 5 , 3 , 4 , 3 , 6 , 1 , 5 , 4 , 2 , 3 , 4 , 5 , 2 , 4 , 5 , 5 , 3 , 4 , 6
4, 2 , 5 , 3 , 5 , 2 , 4 , 3 , 4 , 1 , 3 , 4 , 4 , 1 , 5 , 2 , 4 , 5 , 3 , 4

a) In the space below group together the results in a frequency table.

b) What percentage of the houses have 3 or more residents? ....

Sorting Data 1 & 2 (cont)

4 The test results for a group of students are given below.

Group the data to complete the frequency table below.

31	61	40	63	65
78	52	57	15	35
77	11	68	46	68
64	70	26	87	49

Test Mark	Tally	Frequency
0-19	II	2
20-39		
40-59		
60-79		
80-99		

5 John has recorded the temperature at midday every day for the month of June using a thermometer.

All the temperatures are to the nearest degree Celsius.

a) Group together John's results by completing the frequency table.

Temperature (°C)	Tally	Frequency
$5 \leqslant T < 10$		
$10 \leqslant T < 15$		
$15 \leqslant T < 20$		
$20 \leqslant T < 25$		

b) What percentage of the recorded midday temperatures in June are 15°C or more?

....

6 Bolton Wanderers scored the following number of goals in Premier League matches for the 2002/2003 s
1, 1, 1, 1, 2, 1, 1, 0, 1, 1, 1, 1, 4, 1, 0, 1, 0, 1, 4
0, 0, 0, 1, 0, 1, 4, 1, 1, 0, 2, 1, 2, 0, 1, 0, 2, 0, 2
Group together the data in a frequency table.

7 Emma decided to measure the height (h) of all the students in her class.
Here are the results, to the nearest cm:
171, 178, 166, 173, 180, 173, 186, 176, 170, 184, 178, 174, 169, 189, 175, 182, 181, 171, 179, 164, 178,
191, 169, 178, 173, 188, 167, 192.

a) Sort the data into a frequency table using class intervals $160 \leqslant h < 165$, $165 \leqslant h < 170$ etc.
b) What percentage of the students in Emma's class have a height measurement of 170cm or more?

8 The individual weights of 40 people, to the nearest kg, are as follows:
79, 75, 68, 70, 83, 72, 81, 89, 61, 74, 80, 51, 84, 63, 73, 54, 76, 74, 80, 85, 94, 77, 71, 81, 70, 66, 87, 62, 59
67, 75, 81, 80, 78, 60, 77, 61, 75.
Sort the data into a frequency table using appropriate class intervals.

Sorting Data 3

1 **The following data shows the ages (in years) of 30 shoppers in a supermarket.**

41 , 51 , 8 , 60 , 21 , 31 , 41 , 17 , 68 , 28 , 34 , 45 , 46 , 52 , 74 ,
56 , 10 , 23 , 47 , 30 , 34 , 9 , 42 , 29 , 55 , 44 , 38 , 57 , 47 , 58

Using tens to form the 'stem' and units to form the 'leaves', draw a stem and leaf diagram to show the data.

2 **A survey of 120 people was conducted to find out if they listen to the radio whilst driving.**
Complete the two-way table to show the results.

	Men	Women	Total
Listen to radio	32		73
Do not listen to radio		24	
Total	55		

3 **A survey of 200 Year 7, 8 and 9 pupils was carried out to find their favourite type of music from a choice of three: Pop, Rap or Dance.**

a) Complete the two-way table to show the results.

	Year 7	Year 8	Year 9	Total
Pop	42		18	
Rap		12		41
Dance	14		31	69
Total			62	

b) What percentage of the pupils chose Pop as their favourite type of music?

4 Here are the heights, to the nearest cm, of 30 students in a class:
171, 178, 166, 173, 180, 173, 186, 176, 170, 184, 178, 174, 169, 189, 175, 182, 181, 171, 179, 164, 178, 175, 174, 191, 169, 178, 173, 188, 167, 192.
a) Using tens to form the 'stem' and units to form the 'leaves' draw a stem and leaf diagram to show the data.
b) What is the modal class of the data?
c) What is the median value of the data?

Displaying Data 1

1 A survey was carried out to find the favourite type of music for a group of people. The results are displayed in this pictogram.

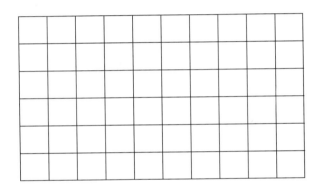

Country
Pop
Classical
Jazz
Rock

represents four people.

Draw a bar graph to show this information.

2 36 primary school children were asked to name their favourite pet.

$\frac{1}{3}$ said DOG

$\frac{1}{4}$ said CAT

$\frac{2}{9}$ said FISH

$\frac{1}{12}$ said RABBIT

... and the remainder said BIRD.

Draw a bar graph to show this information.

3 This bar chart shows the different types of milk sold in a supermarket and the actual number of pints sold on one day.

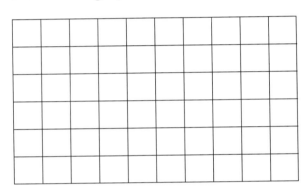

Pints Sold

Types of Milk

a) What was the second most popular type of milk sold?

....

b) How many pints of milk were sold in total?

....

c) In the space below draw a pictogram to show this data.

4 **Draw a)** a pictogram and **b)** a bar graph to show the data recorded in question **2** on page 121.

5 **Draw a)** a pictogram and **b)** a bar graph to show the data recorded in question **3** on page 121.

Displaying Data 2 & 3

1 A group of factory workers were asked how long it took them to get to work.

This table shows the results. Construct a frequency diagram to show this information.

Time, t (minutes)	Number of workers i.e. Frequency
0 ⩽ t < 10	21
10 ⩽ t < 20	14
20 ⩽ t < 30	28
30 ⩽ t < 40	8
40 ⩽ t < 50	4

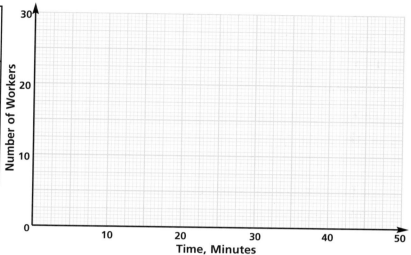

2 In a survey 50 women were asked how much they spend on cosmetics in one week.

The results are shown in the table below.

Money Spent, M (£)	Frequency
0 ⩽ M < 2	1
2 ⩽ M < 4	6
4 ⩽ M < 6	28
6 ⩽ M < 8	11
8 ⩽ M < 10	4

a) Draw a frequency polygon to show the information.

b) 50 men were also asked how much they spend on cosmetics in one week. The results are shown below. On the same axes draw a frequency polygon to show the money spent by men.

Money Spent, M (£)	Frequency
0 ⩽ M < 2	13
2 ⩽ M < 4	28
4 ⩽ M < 6	5
6 ⩽ M < 8	3
8 ⩽ M < 10	1

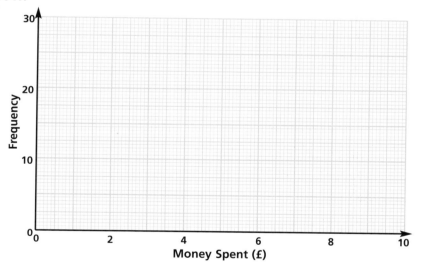

c) How do the two distributions compare?

....

....

....

....

....

....

....

....

....

....

Displaying Data 2 & 3 (cont)

3 The table shows the height of a girl from birth to age 5. Her height was recorded every year on her birthday.

Time (years)	0	1	2	3	4	5
Height (cm)	42	51	66	75	84	89

a) Draw a time series to show the trend in her height.

b) Between which time period was there the greatest increase in height?

....

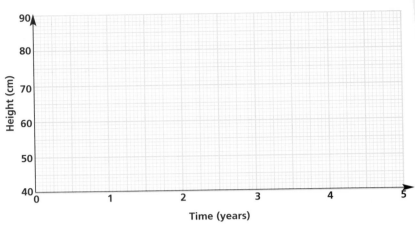

4 The graph below shows the sales of ice-cream at a shop at a seaside resort. What trend, if any, does the graph show?

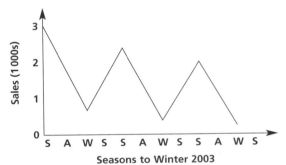

....
....
....
....
....
....
....
....
....
....

5 The table below shows the sales of shoes at a store over a six month period. Use a three point moving average to determine if there is a trend in sales.

Apr	May	Jun	Jul	Aug	Sept
103	78	83	73	57	122

....
....
....
....
....
....
....

6 Below are the highest recorded temperatures, in °C, on one particular day for forty places around the world.

17, 28, 33,19, 21, 28, 31, 24, 21, 20, 19, 28, 24, 19, 20, 24, 29, 32, 16, 26,
33, 24, 23, 16, 16, 20, 28, 17, 24, 23, 26, 31, 33, 18, 31, 26, 28, 19, 19, 21

a) Group together the data in a frequency table.
b) Construct a frequency diagram to show the data.
c) On separate axes construct a frequency polygon to show the data.

Histograms

1 This table shows the distance that the workers at Barney's Biscuits have to travel to work.

   a) Complete the frequency density column in the table.

   b) Draw a histogram to illustrate the data in the table.

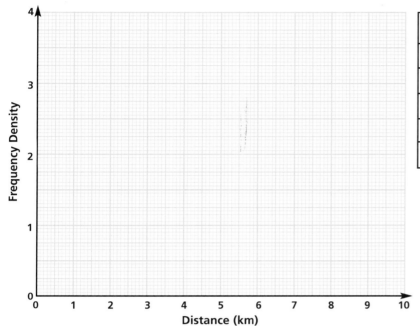

Distance (km)	Freq.	Freq. Density
0 ≤ d < 2	7	3.5
2 ≤ d < 3	3	
3 ≤ d < 4	4	
4 ≤ d < 5	2	
5 ≤ d < 10	8	

2 This histogram shows the distribution of the number of hours that pupils in Kim's class spent on a coursework task. How many pupils are there in Kim's class?

....

....

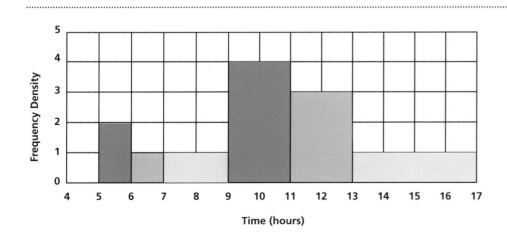

3 The pupils from Whitehall School took part in a fun run for charity. The table shows the times the pupils took to complete the run.

Time (mins)	40 ≤ t < 60	60 ≤ t < 70	70 ≤ t < 80	80 ≤ t < 90	90 ≤ t < 100	100 ≤ t < 120
Frequency	28	43	58	40	34	18

Draw a histogram to illustrate this data.

Scatter Diagrams 1 & 2

1 This scatter diagram shows the average journey time and distance travelled for ten pupils travelling from home to school.

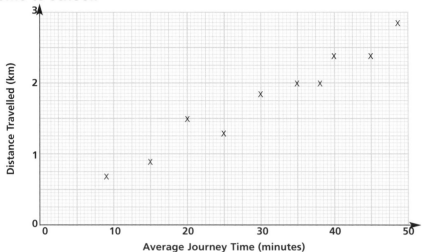

a) What does the scatter diagram tell you about the relationship between the journey time and the distance travelled?

....

b) Draw a line of best fit.

c) Use your graph to estimate ...

i) the time taken by John who travelled a distance of 2.5 km. ....

ii) the distance travelled by Donna who took 27 minutes. ....

2 The table below shows the heights and weights of 10 boys.

Height (cm)	133	162	130	163	153
Weight (kg)	70	84	64	87	87

Height (cm)	150	124	141	150	138
Weight (kg)	77	66	79	82	69

a) Use the information given to plot a scatter diagram, including line of best fit.

b) What type of correlation is there between height and weight?

....

c) i) Tony weighs 72kg. Use your graph to estimate his height. ....

ii) Rob is 1.57m tall. Use your graph to estimate his weight. ....

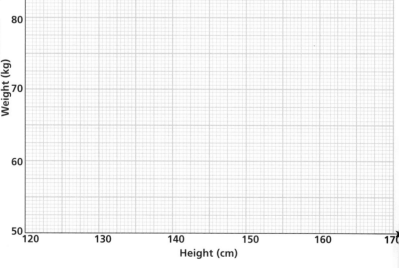

Scatter Diagrams 1 & 2 (cont)

3 Mrs Thrift goes shopping at her local supermarket on 12 separate occasions. Each time she pays for her items with a £10 note. The table below shows the number of items bought and change received.

Change received (£)	2.50	5.60	5.70	7.80	0.90	3.10	5.20	4.20	1.50	7.90	6.80	2.70
Number of items bought	10	8	6	4	14	12	7	8	14	2	7	11

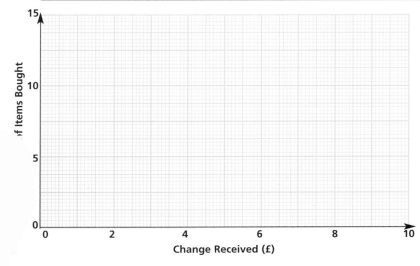

a) Use the information given to plot a scatter diagram including line of best fit.

b) What type of correlation does the scatter diagram show? ....

c) i) Mrs Thrift buys 9 items. Estimate how much change she receives. ....

ii) Mrs Thrift receives £6.20 in change. Estimate how many items she bought.

....

4 The table below shows the number of tracks and total playing time for 12 music CDs.

Number of tracks	14	20	8	11	18	14
Total time (mins)	62	69	58	61	66	67

Number of tracks	10	5	16	7	18	6
Total time (mins)	56	46	66	56	69	52

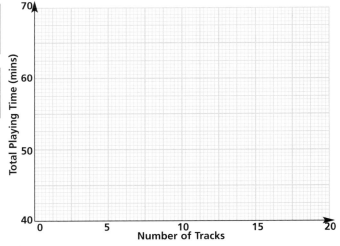

a) Use the information given to plot a scatter diagram, including line of best fit.

b) i) If a CD has 13 tracks, estimate its total playing time. ....

ii) If the total playing time of a CD is 54 minutes, estimate the number of tracks it has. ....

5 The table below gives information about the number of chapters and the total number of pages in the books on Diane's shelf.

Number of chapters	19	28	11	14	27	23	8	16	21	25	32	19	35	11	16
Total number of pages	250	355	110	230	235	350	145	200	235	315	325	120	395	125	305

a) Use the information given to plot a scatter diagram, including line of best fit.
b) What does the scatter diagram tell you about the relationship between the number of chapters and total number of pages?
c) Use your graph to estimate ...
i) the total number of pages if a book has 24 chapters, **ii)** the number of chapters if a book has a total of 190 pages.

Pie Charts

1 **In one week a travel agent sold 120 separate holidays.**

The table below shows the holiday destinations.

Holiday destination	No. of Holidays Sold
Spain	42
Greece	12
France	34
Cyprus	22
Italy	10

a) Draw and label a pie chart to represent these destinations.

b) What percentage of the holidays sold were for Spain?

....

c) What fraction of the holidays sold were for Greece?

....

2 **Rose has completed 40 pieces of work in maths in one school year. Her grades are as follows:**

B, C, A, B, C, D, B, C, B, E, D,
A, B, C, D, B, C, B, B, D, A, C,
C, B, A, D, A, C, B, C, B, A, D,
E, C, B, C, C, B, D.

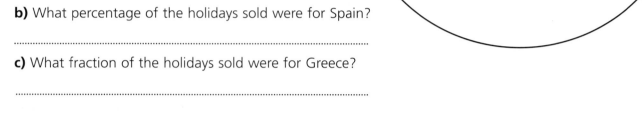

a) Draw a table to show the distribution of grades.

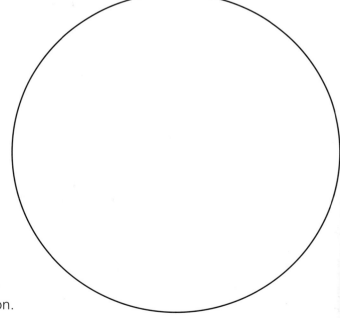

b) Draw and label a pie chart to show the distribution.

c) What fraction of Rose's grades are A's or B's?

....

Pie Charts (cont)

3 **60 men and 60 women were asked, 'What is your favourite colour of car?'**

The two pie charts show the results.

a) i) How many men chose red as their favourite colour?

....

ii) How many women chose red as their favourite colour?

....

b) Did more men or women choose green as their

favourite colour? Show your working.

....

....

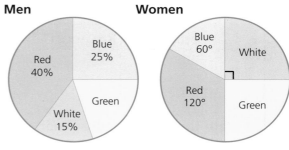

Men **Women**

4 **This pie chart shows the daily newspapers bought by 72 people.**

a) i) Which is the most popular newspaper?

....

ii) Which is the least popular newspaper?

....

b) i) How many people buy the Daily Stir?

....

ii) How many more people buy The National

compared to News Today?

....

---

5 **This table shows the number of telephone calls Mrs Chattergee makes in one week.**

Day of the week	Monday	Tuesday	Wednesday	Thursday	Friday	Saturday	Sunday
Number of phone calls	3	2	8	4	7	10	6

a) Draw and label a pie chart to represent the information.
b) What percentage of the telephone calls were made at the weekend?

6 **The ages of the people living in Addick Close are as follows:**
2, 24, 14, 8, 70, 15, 19, 31, 85, 4, 3, 12, 30, 27, 45, 50, 66, 68, 2, 11,
74, 31, 63, 28, 41, 47, 51, 14, 18, 83, 69, 7, 52, 35, 33, 20, 14, 6, 7, 5.
a) Construct a frequency table to show the distribution of ages using class intervals of 1-20, 21-40, etc.
b) Draw and label a pie chart to show the distribution. **c)** What percentage of the residents are aged 41 or over?

7 **A group of men and women were asked how they travel to work.**
The two pie charts show their responses. They are not drawn accurately.
a) If 10 men travel to work by car, how many men travel to work by ...
i) bus? **ii)** train?
b) If 20 women travel to work by train, how many women travel to work by ...
i) car? **ii)** bus?

Men **Women**

Mean, Median, Mode & Range 1

1 Laura has the following coins in her pocket:

Calculate the mean, median, mode and range for the coins.

Mean: ....

....

Median: .... **Mode:** .... **Range:** ....

2 The table below shows the results of an Internet search for the price of a particular camera.

Calculate the mean, median, mode and range of the camera prices.

Camera	Cost (£)	Camera	Cost (£)	Camera	Cost (£)	Camera	Cost (£)	Camera	Cost (£)
1	227	5	169	9	225	13	211	17	155
2	246	6	204	10	210	14	248	18	153
3	248	7	220	11	239	15	166	19	196
4	248	8	165	12	227	16	170	20	173

Mean: ....

....

Median: .... **Mode:** .... **Range:** ....

3 The weights of the 11 players in the Year 11 hockey team were measured.

Their weights in kilograms were: **51, 60, 62, 47, 53, 48, 52, 51, 65, 61, 66**

a) Calculate the mean, median, mode and range for their weights.

Mean: ....

....

Median: .... Mode: .... Range: ....

b) The weights of the 11 players in the Year 10 hockey team were also measured.

Their mean was 52.5kg and the range was 11kg. Compare the weights of the two teams.

....

....

4 9A contains 14 girls. Their heights in metres are:
1.46, 1.62, 1.57, 1.6, 1.39, 1.71, 1.53, 1.62, 1.58, 1.40, 1.46, 1.63, 1.62, 1.65
   a) Calculate the mean, median, mode and range for the heights.
   b) The boys in 9A have a mean height of 1.68m and a range of 0.32m. Compare the heights of the girls and the boys.

Mean, Median, Mode & Range 2 & 3

1 Janet carries out a survey on the number of passengers in cars which pass her house.

The results are shown in the table.

Number of passengers	Frequency	Frequency x No. of passengers
0	11	
1	12	
2	6	
3	8	
4	3	

a) How many cars were there in her survey?..................................

b) What is the modal number of passengers? ....

c) What is the median number of passengers?..........................

d) What is the range of the number of passengers?................

e) What is the mean number of passengers?

....

....

....

2 This graph shows the number of chocolate bars bought by pupils at a school tuck shop.

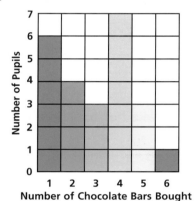

Number of Pupils

Number of Chocolate Bars Bought

a) How many pupils bought chocolate bars? ....

b) What is the modal number of bars bought? ....

c) What is the median number of bars bought? ....

d) What is the mean number of bars bought?

....

....

....

3 The table gives the recorded midday temperature for every day in June.

a) Complete the table and work out an estimate of the mean recorded temperature.

Temperature, T (°C)	Frequency	Mid-temp values (°C)	Frequency x Mid-temp values
5 ≤ T < 10	3	7.5	3 x 7.5 = 22.5
10 ≤ T < 15	14	12.5	
15 ≤ T < 20	11		
20 ≤ T < 25	2		

b) In which class interval does the median lie?..

c) What is the modal class? ....

Mean, Median, Mode & Range 2 & 3

4 Phil carries out a survey about the amount of pocket money his classmates each receive every week. The results are shown below.

Amount of pocket money, M (£)	Frequency		
$0 \leqslant M < 2$	3		
$2 \leqslant M < 4$	15		
$4 \leqslant M < 6$	8		
$6 \leqslant M < 8$	5		
$8 \leqslant M < 10$	1		

a) Calculate an estimate of the mean amount of pocket money the pupils receive.

....

....

b) In which class interval does the median lie? ....

c) What is the modal class? ....

5 This graph shows the amount of time Narisha had to wait for a bus to take her to school each morning for half a term.

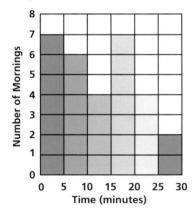

a) How many mornings are shown altogether? ....

....

b) Calculate an estimate of the mean amount of time Narisha had to wait for a bus.

....

....

....

....

6 The table below shows the number of goals scored by the Year 11 football team in one season.

Number of goals scored	0	1	2	3	4	5	6
Number of games	7	5	11	3	3	0	1

a) What is **i)** the mean **ii)** the range **iii)** the mode **iv)** the median of the number of goals scored?
b) The Year 10 football team averaged 2.2 goals per game in five less games. Which year scored the most goals and by how many?

7 During a PE lesson the boys had a 100m race. Their times were recorded and the results are shown below.

Time taken, t(seconds)	$12 < t \leqslant 14$	$14 < t \leqslant 16$	$16 < t \leqslant 18$	$18 < t \leqslant 20$	$20 < t \leqslant 22$	$22 < t \leqslant 24$
Number of boys	2	9	13	5	3	1

a) Calculate an estimate of the mean time
b) In which class interval does the median lie?
c) Which is the modal class?

Cumulative Frequency 1 & 2

1 This cumulative frequency graph shows the time taken for 30 pupils to complete their maths homework.

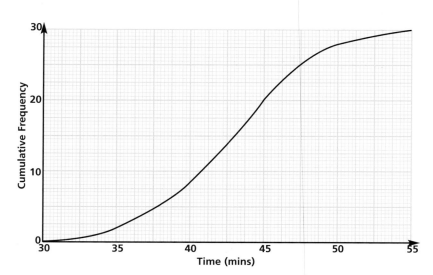

a) How many pupils took less than 40 minutes?

....

b) How many pupils took more than 40 minutes?

....

c) What was the median time taken?

....

2 Thirty five people took part in a skateboarding competition. The points they scored are shown in the table below.

Points Scored (P)	Frequency	Cumulative Frequency
0 < P ≤ 5	2	
5 < P ≤ 10	4	
10 < P ≤ 15	5	
15 < P ≤ 20	7	
20 < P ≤ 25	12	
25 < P ≤ 30	5	

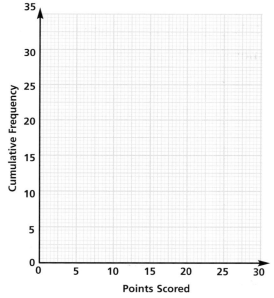

a) Complete the cumulative frequency column in the table.

b) Draw the cumulative frequency graph.

c) Use the graph to estimate ...

i) the median points scored ....

ii) the inter-quartile range ....

d) How many competitors scored between 15 and 25 points?

....

e) How many competitors scored more than 25 points?

....

....

Cumulative Frequency 1 & 2 (cont)

3 The cumulative frequency graph shows the Resistant Materials test results for 80 boys. The test was out of 50.

a) What was the median result?

....

b) What was the inter-quartile range?

....

c) How many boys scored more than 45?

....

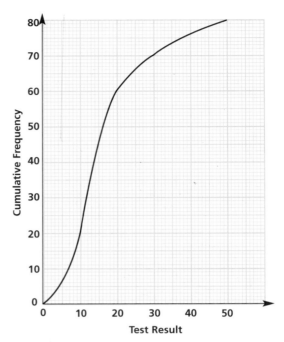

d) 80 girls also completed the test. The table below shows their results. Complete the table.

Test Result (T)	Frequency	Cumulative Frequency
0 < T ≤ 10	4	
10 < T ≤ 20	13	
20 < T ≤ 30	19	
30 < T ≤ 40	34	
40 < T ≤ 50	10	

e) Draw the cumulative frequency curve for the girls on the same graph.

f) What was the median result for the girls?

....

g) How do the two sets of results compare? Use two readings to support your comparisons.

....

....

....

....

4 The heights in cm of 300 pupils were recorded as shown.
a) Complete the table, adding a cumulative frequency column.
b) Draw the cumulative frequency curve on a graph.
c) Use your graph to find the ...
i) Median height ii) inter-quartile range iii) number of pupils taller than 155cm.

Height (h)	Frequency
130 < h ≤ 140	10
140 < h ≤ 150	39
150 < h ≤ 160	95
160 < h ≤ 170	125
170 < h ≤ 180	31

5 In one week a doctor weighed 80 men. The table shows the results.

Weight	50 < W ≤ 60	60 < W ≤ 70	70 < W ≤ 80	80 < W ≤ 90	90 < W ≤ 100
Frequency	11	27	29	8	5

a) Draw a cumulative frequency curve on a graph.
b) Use your graph to estimate the ...
i) median weight ii) inter-quartile range
c) What percentage of men weighed more than 70kg?